OUTNUMBERED and too often outmaneuvered as we are in the Cold War, our program must become a massive offensive with the one weapon for which Russia has no anti-missile defense: the Christian faith and its power to make us all fit to live together in one world.

The Ultimate Weapon

–CHRISTIANITY

**THE CASE FOR A FOREIGN POLICY
OF MILITANT CHRISTIANITY**

PAUL M. STEVENS

RADIO AND TELEVISION COMMISSION
of the Southern Baptist Convention
Ft. Worth, Texas

Paperback Edition published, April, 1966
by the Radio and Television Commission
of the Southern Baptist Convention

Original Edition published by Thomas Nelson and Sons, 1961

Library of Congress Catalog Card No.: 61-7748

PRINTED IN THE UNITED STATES OF AMERICA

Onward Christian Soldiers

Marching as to war

With the Cross of Jesus

Going on before

Introduction

The Radio and Television Commission of the Southern Baptist Convention re-issues "The Ultimate Weapon—Christianity," written by Dr. Paul M. Stevens, executive director of the Commission, in this paperback edition for several reasons.

First, we believe that Communism will always be the avowed enemy of Christianity, and that it poses an even greater threat to our world than it did five years ago when this book was published by Thomas Nelson and Sons in 1961.

The book contains an urgent challenge to all Christians, and especially to laymen, to give themselves more fully to Jesus Christ and His Kingdom on earth. We want *this* pertinent message for our day available to as many readers as possible.

Its presentation of a practical plan for fighting Communism with the West's greatest weapon—Christianity—makes it a timeless and important book in any age. It remains as fresh as the gospel it seeks to open to the world. It is reminiscent of the message of the prophets of old, calling for repentance and reform, as it calls for a new approach to Christian missions to meet the needs of the Space Age.

Believing in the ultimate power of the Christian message then, we reprint this important and challenging book which cites revolutionary Christianity as the force which can win the world. As the author states so well:

> One can come to only one honest conclusion. If man is a spiritual being, whose crucial needs of this hour can only be met with spiritual resources, and if there is a sense of emergency hanging over world affairs and even the existence of our nation, then we must find a way of matching the material and political contributions of our nation with dynamic and farsighted action in the spiritual realm on a scale never before attempted by the Christian people of the world. If there is the will, God will provide the way.

Christianity, Dr. Stevens eloquently argues, was once the world's most feared idea. It burst on the ancient world like a bomb with chain reactions, and ideas that were in conflict with it were destroyed.

Today, however, Western influence lacks the explosive force of the world's most feared idea. Now is the time for Christians in America to mount an offensive of gigantic militant proportions against the world's second most feared idea—Communism.

Dr. Stevens spells out a strategy for a Christian foreign policy, one that takes advantage of factors in our favor and provides for long-range planning for 50 years. Problems of personnel, literature, supplies, timing, languages, and organization are discussed, and coordination with State and Business is envisioned. Here is a practical plan on the grand scale for carrying out Christ's injunction: "Go ye into all the world and preach the gospel to every creature."

Contents

✳✳✳✳✳✳✳✳✳✳✳✳✳✳✳✳

ix

The Ultimate Weapon—

CHRISTIANITY

Ideas Are Bombs

SINCE IN THIS BOOK WE ARE RECOMMENDING PREMEDITATED
war on an all-out, massive, world-wide scale, it is likely that
the argument will be of more than passing interest to all
financial, economic and industrial circles in our world as well
as to every parent or potential parent. That this war is to be
mounted preventively should not change one's attitude toward its importance. Nor should one be dismayed at the
possibility of providing the enemy with information by
which he can adequately protect himself from attack. For
the type of war we recommend and the kind of enemy we
face, no counter-preparation is feared or even possible. The
enemy is unprepared and vulnerable now, and will remain
so until we strike and win. We shall announce our methods
and goals and find our enemy unable to believe we mean
business and thus he will remain unprepared for the
attack.

The war we recommend will be fought successfully by
the type of all-out mobilization that was used to make America capable of fighting successfully in 1941–45. This mobilization will call for the concentration of brains, skills, food,

clothing and equipment in massive quantities, with dedication and desperation marking the attitude and efforts of all who are thrown into the battle.

As you have guessed by now, we are not talking about a war of violence, though as of this moment, that is the only kind of war we are capable of fighting. But fortunately that kind of war is more than likely obsolete. Its obsolescence grows out of mutual fear on the part of the potential enemies. Suffice it to say that those who know the true consequences of a war of violence predict that such a war would be the last act of civilization on this planet.

Warfare of some kind is inevitable in a divided world such as we have at present. Not only is it inevitable but to a degree it is going on around us at this moment. It is the war of ideas. As the Fifth Columns infiltrated Austria and Norway during the early part of World War II and those countries were delivered to the enemy with comparatively little struggle, so we are being deceived, misled and weakened by internal forces just as powerful today.

We do not mean that there is no struggle on our part to defend ourselves. The struggle is as intense and desperate as our political leaders who are awake can make it. It is just that we cannot hope to win with the type of weapons we now use. It is true that blockbuster "bombs" in the form of powerful ideas are being dropped on the nations of the world with fearful rapidity and consequences by both sides. The novelty and the imagination involved in the construction of these "bombs" again and again has caught one side or the other off guard.

From our arsenal of weapons we produced a "bomb" called the Marshall Plan. Its consequences are still being felt throughout the world. Then the Russians fired off their "Peaceful Co-existence" missile. Before we could recover from the blow they blasted us with "Let Us Compete." We retaliated with "Open Skies Policy" and "Atoms For Peace," just to name a few. Then Khrushchev came to the U.N. to drop another earthshaker, "Total Disarmament." Then he torpedoed the summit conference.

Some rather foggy thinking led some of our fellow men to label the 1960 Paris summit collapse as a U. S. Foreign Policy failure. This, of course, is not true. That "summit" collapsed on that nameless day when in the secret enclaves of the Kremlin-criminals, it was decided that the "co-existence" phase of the Foreign Policy of Russia under Khrushchev had not succeeded in deceiving the Free World. The Paris Conference was doomed from that day, regardless of Eisenhower or the U-2 incident.

Nothing could better illustrate this free-wheeling type of attack by the enemy than the spectacular success which the Soviets managed to wring out of a foregone Foreign Policy failure. As in any "military-type assault," they found an opening and an appropriate weapon, and they made the most of it!

The student of the daily newspapers and weekly magazines would have no difficulty in naming many more of the huge "vehicles of destruction" that have been thrown by both sides in this war for men's minds. Nor would this same student disagree with the apparent fact that Russia has dropped more and bigger "bombs" than has the Western World. Not because they possess superior weapons or superior ability, but simply because we have been unable to accomplish at least two steps:

1. To get our Western World united in the recognition
   that the struggle in which we are involved is a matter of life and death, and
2. Refuse to let the enemy continually choose the battlefields upon which he wishes to fight, and the
   weapons with which we therefore are forced to
   fight.

For anyone may see that Russia thus far has chosen the
underdeveloped countries of the world as the battlefield and
she has chosen the promise of food, military equipment and
machinery, as well as threats of war, as the weapons. And
so far, to a large extent, these have comprised the elements
of the only front on which we have waged any battle.

Though Russia has not always lived up to all her promises
of wheat, money and equipment to her needy "friends,"
honesty compels us to say that the truth of the matter is
that she can match us, sack of wheat for sack of wheat, dollar for dollar, and machine for machine. With the Communistic World's resources focused on out-expanding and out-
producing us in the material realm, there are many people
today who privately admit that we cannot win. The percen-
tages are against it. Unless some sort of internal catastrophe
occurs, the Communists are slated to win this kind of war.
We cannot rely on what "may happen." The fact of the
moment is that we are fighting a losing battle on their chosen
battlefield with their chosen weapons.

The confusion of the "defenders" of Christian righteousness was never more clearly illustrated than in the wave of
weakness and the medley of appeasing and critical voices
that arose across this country during and immediately after

the ill-fated 1960 Paris Conference referred to above. In a fight for our very existence, at a time when every resource of Christian courage was to be marshaled for the cause of peace and strength, we had to sit and witness the peculiar behavior of political and spiritual leaders weeping in despair. Watch them as they, like dogs of doom, pointed their collective muzzles at the refuse cans of some remote alley of American life and then lifted their thin heads to howl at some distant and dismal moon.

Thus, if we lose battles to these evil men in Russia, it is not altogether because their choice of weapons and battle-fields is superior to ours. It is undoubtedly partially due to a great spiritual weakness on the part of the West: weakness in the one area in which we must be strong, or else.

Up to this point, we have found ourselves spending our time and efforts in a constant "changing of posture." In other words, we have been attempting to roll with the blows and to be prepared to retaliate instantaneously. But this retalia-tion is chiefly in the field of atomic warfare which we know and Russia knows none of us can afford to unleash. And while we have shifted and turned to face each "bomb rattling" speech of Stalin or Khrushchev, they, in the meantime, have never seriously intended to get involved in an atomic war anywhere. Instead they have literally bombarded us almost off the face of the earth with "ideas." They have not been reasonable or factual ideas nor have they been even honestly presented. But they have been thrown at us with the whole world looking on, and the whole world has wondered and marveled at the success of the Russian Bear over the Amer-ican Eagle.

And with the whole world looking on, another strange

thing has happened to prove our point. In the last ten years
the Communists have carried out a series of offensives such
as:

1. Attritional guerrilla warfare in Malaya and Vietnam
2. Attritional ground warfare in Korea
3. Military or political support of anti-western guerrilla
   movements in Algeria, Lebanon, Aden and Cyprus
4. Infiltration and partial occupation of Burmese and
   Cambodian territory
5. Virtual annexation of Tibet
6. Paramilitary-political infiltration of Laos
7. Political infiltration into the governments of Indonesia, Syria and Iraq
8. Assumption of power via the ballot box in Kerala,
   India.

In every instance cited above where the Russians or the
Communists have been challenged to "stop or else" they have
stopped! Actually, except in the case of Korea, World War
III has not even been seriously threatened. Not once has
the challenge been picked up.

Even in the case of the invasion of Egypt by France and
England in 1957, the type of event that would have been
made to order for a Hitler or a Mussolini, Russia has rattled
her bombs at the West, and little more.

Now, in spite of this obvious fact, with its repeated under-
scorings in just this past decade alone, we still react with
the regularity of Pavlov's famous dog, by almost falling into
a state of paralysis when the possibility of an atomic war
is threatened. To be even more accurate, so defensive has
the Western mentality become that intellectual leaders in

almost all the Western Countries tend to write off Communistic expansionism, both its successes and its threats. To many of them the risks involved in a policy of "prevention by intervention" outweigh the value of the real estate and population which the Russians have nibbled away in these 15 years. Their assumptions are false in two places:

1. War with Communism need not take place on non-communist territory alone.
2. We are not "containing" the Communists. They are actually containing us. To how many of our leaders has it occurred that we *may* not be on the outside, looking in. We may be on the inside looking out!

Of course, Communism is convinced that the last is true. The Communist is convinced that whatever revolutionary forces once charged the air and sparked the activity of the free nations of the world have now died down to a harmless glow. He is confident of clear-cut victory. He bases his confidence on two things:

1. Sheer numbers are on his side, since he claims to control, in one way or another, two out of every three people on earth.
2. The new always destroys and builds on the decline of the old.

Writer Yu Chao-li wrote in the Communist paper *Red Flag* on August 16, 1958, "Today the last bastions of imperialism are being shaken violently by the irresistible popular revolutionary forces. The billion people of the Socialist camp now have at their side in the struggle against imperialism the more than 700 million people of the former colonial countries which have already won their independence. In addition, there are the 600 million people in the countries which are still fighting for independence or full independence . . . in human history, the forces of the new always defeat the forces of decay. New emergent forces, though seemingly weak, always prevail over the old, moribund forces which are still seemingly strong. What is decaying will inevitably be replaced by the new-born. Such is the law of development and in society."

So says the enemy. All his points are probably correct. Civilizations that are old and inflexible, have been overthrown by the young and revolutionary over and over again in the world history. So? So it behooves us to look carefully to see if we, economically and spiritually, have reached the place that Mr. Yo Chao-li says we have. Is he speaking truthfully or is he speaking wishfully?

Our faith was born as a revolt. A revolt against the entrenched and evil powers in the economic and spiritual areas.

Rome, proud, haughty and expansive, was ready to be challenged and overthrown. She had grown old and inflexible. The Jews that composed the Priestly Sect in Jerusalem had reached the same point of inflexibility. Defenders of the status quo, they were. And when the revolutionary movement called Christianity challenged them, they fell.

Christianity *was* a revolutionary movement. In order for us to determine whether it still is, we must try to define a revolutionary movement. Such a definition must of necessity, in this case, be in the simplest possible terms.

Every revolutionary movement, such as was Christianity in the first century, must first rely more on its breadth of vision than on its potential power in order to assure final victory. Its strategy rests upon a superior understanding of its final goal and the total historic situation rather than a grasp of the status quo. The spectrum of its activities must be as wide as the total scale of social change desired. Not only that, but a Central Intelligence capable of phasing the instruments and areas of conflict, whether they be economic, political, psychological or technological, must be set up to organize the planned conflict or conflicts. That Central Intelligence must see itself as the aggressor and choose its weapons accordingly, while the defender of status quo only sees the tools of "peace." In short, the aggressive revolutionary turns plowshares into swords to accomplish his purpose.

The Christian movement in the early days was characterized by each of these requirements:

1. It had a breadth of vision that included the entire population of the world.
2. Its areas and methods of attack covered the broadest spectrum of possibilities consistent with its motives and goals.
3. Its choice of weapons was unique in variety and composition.
4. Its central intelligence claimed omnipotence and the followers had complete confidence that it was so.
5. World-wide victory was an accomplished fact to these men, even before the conflict began.

The vision of the Christian movement was fixed on the whole world by Christ, and carried out in its first stages by Paul the Apostle. Christ had stated this in no uncertain terms when He said to His disciples on the occasion of His ascension, "Go into all the world and preach the gospel to the whole creation." And Paul openly stated his belief that he was called to be an apostle to the whole Gentile world.

Here was the first sign that a true revolution was under way. And when the dispersion of the Christians took place during the great persecution that broke out against the Church, they were scattered like sparks from a fire when one seeks to put it out by stamping it with his feet (Acts 8:1). Thus the first cadre of revolutionaries of Christianity spread throughout the civilized world.

Its areas and methods of attack were varied and seemed to the Romans and Jews as endless. When Stephen was stoned to death in Jerusalem, a fire was lighted, not extinguished (Acts 7:59). When Paul found himself in serious trouble, he pulled out the fact of his Roman citizenship and using that "passport" got into the very household of Caesar in Rome (Acts 22:25–30). Churches or assemblies were formed that met in the people's homes and secret signs were developed, such as the sign of the fish, whereby believers could identify themselves to one another safely. When they were thrown into jail, the jailer oftentimes was converted as in the case of the Philippian jailer (Acts 16:25–34). And not only jailers but the prisoners themselves as in the case of Onesimus the runaway slave (Philemon).

They fought on the economic front also as in the instance of the silversmiths in Ephesus (Acts 19). And the young girl who supposedly possessed the spirit of divination (Acts 16), and whose activities were the source of much gain for her masters.

They climbed over walls, escaped from prison, worked miracles, preached non-violent overthrow of evil, and in fact every situation became a preaching situation; thus they carried the opportunities of attack to the furthest possible limits.

Then the choice of weapons. Whoever heard of fighting a revolution with Love? How could you fight a movement whose leader was believed to have risen from the dead and who appeared to his followers? We know about the dead and embalmed bodies of Lenin and Stalin, but here was a leader who refused to lie down and be embalmed! Look at some of the literature they produced. Apocalyptic in form, it was completely unintelligible to the Roman. The stories they told, which they called parables, seemed as harmless as bedtime yarns.

And when these people were thrown to the lions or burned at the stake, they prayed for those who were putting them to death. One of the Roman Centurions who was present at the Crucifixion of Christ was so struck with this man's prayer for his forgiveness, he shouted to the whole world, "This man truly was the Son of God." How can you combat weapons like that?

Every convert to Christianity became obsessed with the desire to win another convert. This, too, was impossible to defeat. The men, the women, the children, all of them. The careful watching of their twelve leaders, called apostles, by Roman officials was easy but can you watch every man on every street in every conversation in which he engages?

They fought with kindness, love and sympathy. They fought in the areas where Rome had failed the most—the areas of human need. To the oppressed, the poor, the imprisoned, the widowed, the sick, the hungry, the world's downcast and underprivileged people, they gave hope. Hope

for a better future. They gave them peace, a peace with God
that seemed impossible to explain or understand, but which
could belong to anyone who would believe.

Its Central Intelligence claimed and proved that it could
foresee events, overcome superior forces and predict the
future. This Central Intelligence was God. He directed them
by visions and dreams. He inspired them by arranging
thrilling escapes for their leaders from enemy prisons (Acts
12) or from sinking ships at sea (Acts 27).

He directed the writing of a sort of "Manifesto," only in-
finitely more honest and more profound. It was composed
of letters which were later to be bound in a volume called
the New Testament, but which now were smuggled through
enemy lines and read in secret by thousands. He managed
to confound the intelligence of the enemy and create confusion among the ranks of enemy followers. He assured
His Christian soldiers that He knew what the ultimate victory was and that He knew how to get there. Thus absolute
confidence was generated in these early "salesmen" of Christianity to such an extent that no matter what Rome did to
throw a scare into them, it didn't work. What can you do
with people like this?

Thus, with worldwide victory in only a matter of time,
they went serenely to their imprisonment or death, if such
was demanded of them. And a smile seemed to be playing
at their lips as they viewed and then prayed for their captors.

Now, if these and other characteristics of the "Revolutionary Movement" called Christianity can be called substantially
correct, where does this same movement stand today? Does
it have the same sources of vitality it once had? What part
of the picture has changed?

Is the battle almost won and have we therefore slowed down a little? No! Emphatically no! On the contrary, we lose ground every day. The battle goes against us.

Has Central Intelligence let us down? Did He die like Lenin or commit suicide like Hitler or was he assassinated like Lincoln?

What about the variety and effectiveness of the weapons? Love—Hope—Forgiveness—the New Testament?

Are our forces fewer than they were in those early days? Is the enemy we fight today more malevolent than then?

Or, to state the problem as a whole: are all the elements intact that made Christianity so powerful and feared in its infancy? If so, and they are, where does the trouble lie?

The trouble simply is this. We have been lulled into a state of lethargy and ease to such an extent that we find ourselves in the vulnerable and indefensible position of acting as defenders of the status quo. Fending off blows and trying to outguess the aggressiveness of our enemy, we have lost the spirit of the revolutionist. Our enemy has taken the initiative away from us. He uses every weapon we once used. He extends hope to the downtrodden, he infiltrates our schools and colleges. He places leaders in high places and claims invincible intelligence. His eye is on the whole world and he proclaims his ultimate victory with a confidence that is so sure, it is frightening. If he is right that we are decadent and benign; if he can convince us that we have occupied the stage long enough; if he can convince us consciously or subconsciously that our beliefs and philosophies are outmoded, then he can win the day, then the battle is already lost. Millions believe it this very moment. And millions more stand for an uncertain moment in "neutralism." Throwing them food at a fantastic rate can hold them on that edge of indecision for a while. But it will not, it cannot, convince them permanently that our way is the best. "Man does not live by bread alone"; he never has and never will. Communism can offer only so much, and planted in what they offer to the people of the world is the seed of our destruction unless we can fight back with something better. We have it. It has been used effectively in the past. It is being used effectively in many, many places today. Here and there on the shore-line of human existence there are small pools of water that are fresh and satisfying. But these pools are unrelated to one another and alone they are small. If only a great tidal wave of Christian concern could sweep in, filling and overflowing and connecting all these isolated pools of life-giving water, then the impact of the saying of Christ, "I came that they may have life, and have it abundantly". (John 10:10, RSV) would come to pass.

Here is the "Idea Bomb" that would, in its chain-reaction, burn out the cancer of Communism and restore the world to being a safe place to live and worship God as we please.

The question is, can Christianity really do this? Again let us return to those early days and re-examine our faith. For there was a time when it was called the *world's most feared idea*. THE WAY!

TWO

The World's Most Feared Idea

THE TITLE OF THIS CHAPTER COULD RECEIVE AT LEAST TWO
interpretations. It could mean that Christianity was really
feared when it was first introduced into the world. Or it
could mean that it only became feared when its threat to the
Roman Empire was recognized.

The answer to questions the reader might raise about the
interpretation can be capsulized in the prophecies of the
Old Testament concerning the hatred of rulers and kings
for Godly rule over the world. One prophecy especially
seems to prove the point. "Why do the nations conspire, and
the peoples plot in vain? The kings of the earth set themselves, and the rulers take counsel together, against the Lord
and his anointed, saying, 'Let us burst their bonds asunder,
and cast their cords from us. He who sits in the heavens
laughs; the Lord has them in derision" (Psalms 2:1–4, RSV).

And then, as if to give a terrible underscoring at the very
beginning of Christ's life, Herod ordered the death of all male
children two years of age and under. In this very act we
see the potential hatred, which later rose to a frenzy, which
the world held toward Christianity.

The persecution and crucifixion of Christ were direct results of the fear of intrenched powers toward "The Way" which He preached. As these Scribes and Pharisees listened to Him openly or clandestinely, they discovered that if an individual or the nation took these teachings seriously, their present exalted position of power would be destroyed. But it was not only the desire to maintain the status quo that gave birth to and then spurred their fear. It was also a belief that the things Jesus did and taught could not answer the needs of the day. For He came preaching non-violence as a means of accomplishing God's will among men. In a fiercely violent world, this philosophy had little or no appeal to the man of power. "Love your enemies, do good to those who hate you" (Luke 6:27, RSV). "From him who takes away your cloak do not withhold your coat as well" (Luke 6:29, RSV). "If any one forces you to go one mile, go with him two miles" (Matthew 5:41, RSV). "Blessed are the peacemakers, for they shall be called sons of God" (Matthew 5:9, RSV). "All who take the sword will perish by the sword" (Matthew 26:52, RSV). "Render therefore to Caesar the things that are Caesar's, and to God the things that are God's" (Matthew 22:21, RSV). These and other teachings of Christ seemed absolutely absurd to the man of power, yet the fearful part was that people were believing these things.

All of it seemed so incongruous and inadequate in the face of world problems. Its simplicity was a mark of inadequacy which they could overlook. One reason for this was the stern fact of life under Roman rule. For the kind of world into which Christ came was a cruel world, a heartless world in which a totalitarian government—Rome—reigned supreme. Its magnificent successes were unquestionable. A system of government and laws which held the major part if not all the

world under its control. A superb road system made Rome
the financial and merchandising center of the world. Great
armies, completely loyal to Rome, occupied the nations of the
world. And the Emperor, by claiming to be a god, had managed actually to center in himself despotic control over the
destinies of almost all men. Out of this absolute power
there arose the beginnings of the ultimate absolute corruption which would one day contribute to the nations' downfall. The Roman world had one vocabulary, Latin; one
army, Caesar's legions; one aim, world solidarity; and one
god, Caesar. Now, into this well-woven scheme of things
steps the harbinger of a new vocabulary, a new army, a new
world aim and a new God—Christianity!

It is no wonder opposition was forthcoming. Some opposition came as a result of one set of reasons, while others
opposed for an entirely different set of reasons. But one does
not need to weigh the reasons behind desperation. It is
enough to know the new force is there. And it was there.
Judaism and the government of Rome, strange bedfellows
indeed, set about to destroy it.

As the enemies of Christianity assessed it, they found
it embodied certain characteristics that, strangely enough,
were parallel with those of Rome:

> Total allegiance
> Refusal to respect national boundaries
> Militancy
> World domination
> Religious fervor
> A new "language"
> New symbols
> Supernaturalism

As these and other important points of similarity were revealed, it became quite evident to the opposition that this concept of man and his relationship to his fellowman and his God was to be greatly feared. For men to believe and follow what Jesus was teaching and what Paul, later, was to preach so eloquently, would be the end of the world that they had so painstakingly put together. The small-scale effort of Rome to crush the "uprising" by crucifying the leader was considered by all to have been the end of the matter. When, however, the supernatural entered into the picture; when the leader refused to stay dead, when He spoke to men and appeared to men from time to time, then they suspected that they had trouble. How *much* trouble they did not know. For this new way of life began rapidly to make inroads into the life stream of the world's greatest power.

First, it was totalitarian in its demands. "You shall love the Lord your God with all your heart, and with all your soul, and with all your strength, and with all your mind . . ." (Luke 10:27, RSV). "If any man would come after me, let him deny himself and take up his cross and follow me" (Matthew 16:24, RSV). "No one can serve two masters; for either he will hate the one and love the other, or he will be devoted to the one and despise the other" (Matthew 6:24, RSV). "No one who puts his hand to the plow and looks back is fit for the kingdom of God" (Luke 9:62, RSV).

Not only did it demand and challenge the *whole* man, it also claimed to change his relationship with other men. A man could not live this Christian life off in a corner. Once Christianity was believed, one was committed to getting others to believe. Thus, the element of religious fervor came into the picture. Every attempt to stamp it out tended only to increase its spread.

Then Rome noticed a new vocabulary and new symbols being used among the people. The cross, so hated and feared by the Romans, became the true symbol of love. Unbelievable! The exact opposite of the meaning which the Romans attached to it. God became a Father, while the Roman gods were feared with superstitious terror. Life in this world was of insignificant importance to the Christian, while to the first century man, it was everything. Money and the getting of wealth were almost spurned by the early day Christian "fanatics." Their leader, Jesus, had not owned a foot of land nor carried a coin in His pocket. He died a pauper and was buried in a borrowed tomb.

Then Rome recognized that these people, the Christ-followers, seemed to have no respect of nationalities or territorial boundaries. It was told them that Christ, upon the occasion of His "resurrection," actually charged His disciples with the task of winning the whole world to their way of thinking. World-wide domination! Global war was to be the plan of attack. No nation, no throne was safe. With great dedication these people became willing to die. They were inspired by supernatural powers that not only made it possible for their leader to appear and converse with them, though He had been crucified, but also granted to their living leaders the power to perform miracles. Rome knew the challenge had been cast at her feet. She picked it up with a viciousness seldom if ever exceeded in all her list of excesses. For Christianity had burst like a bomb in the minds of men.

Total power met total power, militancy met militancy, allegiance met allegiance, and desire for world domination

met this same desire in the enemy. The student of Roman
history will find that on the floor of the Senate, Christianity
was recognized and called the world's most feared idea. It
challenged everything Rome stood for. Its tactics of infiltration, its appeal to the downtrodden, and secret meetings of
what might be called "cells" sent chills through those in power.
Consequently, Rome mounted an offensive seldom, if ever,
equaled in the history of mankind. Wholesale slaughter,
suspension of all laws pertaining to fair trial and punishment,
confiscation of property and attempts toward total suppression, were the orders of every day. And still it spread with
chain-reaction rapidity. Over the very roads Rome had
built, through the strongest barriers she had managed to
erect, it went and even infected men in high places who
had sworn undying allegiance to Rome. There was no way
to stop its progress.

Its teachings cut at the very roots of Roman power. Listen
to some of them:

A living, unseen, yet all powerful, eternal God, revealed in Jesus Christ. "All authority in heaven and on
earth has been given to me" (Matthew 28:18, RSV).

A free man in a free state. "So if the Son makes you
free, you will be free indeed" (John 8:36, RSV).

The personal value of the individual exceeding all
other priorities. "Are not five sparrows sold for two pen-
nies? And not one of them is forgotten before God.
Why, even the hairs of your head are all numbered.
Fear not; you are of more value than many sparrows"
(Luke 12:6–7, RSV).

Allegiance to the living God supersedes all other

claims. "You shall love the Lord your God with all your heart, and with all your soul, and with all your mind" (Matthew 22:37, RSV).

Thus Christianity stood, challenging all comers in every area of life. Every conflicting idea in the world was forced to stand in the arena of men's minds with the world's most feared "idea." And victory was added to victory! Over deserts, mountains, rivers and oceans, it spread, and it brought to defeat all who stood in its path. Not by arms, mind you, and not by means of superior numbers. It merely blew the opposition apart from within! Kings and emperors became believers and whole nations were affected and soon, much sooner than anyone could have possibly believed, it had invaded and made its mark on almost every nation, philosophy and religion in the civilized world.

Never had there been anything like it. The Hindu religion was old when Christianity came, yet it was limited to a rather small area of the world. Buddhism and Confucianism had many of the very same teachings that were later to characterize Christianity, yet they too had a limited following. The philosophies of Greece and the teachings of Judaism were well-known universally, yet they too had remained fairly localized. No moral, legal or ethical body of teachings ever to appear on the earth had so captured men's minds and hearts. History records that fear and pessimism and recognition of ultimate defeat were expressed openly by the powers that existed every time they were faced with the Christian concept. Adaptation and dilution were attempted and in some cases were ingenuously successful for a time. Yet this method was not completely successful.

And so it was that thrones and kingdoms capitulated or were overthrown. In three hundred years the Roman Empire itself fell under the onslaught. Militant Christianity had conquered!

Now the author would be the first to agree that the above picture of the conquest of Christianity had its sorry chapters. It suffered defeats in many ways, small and large. All wasn't rosy by any means. Far from it. Since human instrumentality was involved, the Christian conquest reflected the flaws and faults of men. Efforts to blunt its thrust or weaken its power by adaptation or dilution or misinterpretation, as indicated previously, were fearfully successful in far too many ways and places. Some of the successes in these areas, enjoyed then, remain to plague us to this very day. But no one can deny the fact that the revolutionary spirit in the missionary efforts of early Christianity was responsible for actually doing what seemed to be the impossible. And the student of this accomplishment will be familiar with the fact that from the beginning, opposing forces did not have a chance against so exciting and powerful a concept of a man and his God.

Secondly, I am ready to agree that the "success story" of Christianity is not and never has been actually world-wide. Great areas of the earth, already referred to as the "Hinduistic, Buddhistic and Confucianistic" areas were and still are firmly resistant to Christian teachings as such. The reasons are interesting enough for us to digress for a bit.

Were we to draw a line south from Istanbul (the city once known as Byzantium, and later as Constantinople) and let it pass to the right of the capital of Troy and the island of Rhodes and then slice through the subcontinent of Asia

Minor, we would divide the two great civilizations of ancient times. And this line is as real and factual today as it was 1000 to 1500 years ago. Imaginary and somewhat inaccurate, it represents a real division between two worlds. At one time or another, these "worlds" have sought to invade one another, either by force or by ideologies. Paul the Apostle enjoyed some success in his invasion of the East and Mohammed likewise in the West. But the "bridge" remains today, to a large degree, an unaccomplished challenge. Why?

Herbert J. Muller, in his book, *The Loom of History*, advances the theory that it is the result of a difference in attitudes. In the earliest times, says Mr. Muller, it was a difference in attitude toward the gods and man's relationship with them. Later, it was the difference in view about one man's position in one God's universe. Lest the reader be tempted to place too little importance on that important observation, let me state it again: Man's (collective) attitude toward the gods and his (collective) relationship with them; and one man's position in one God's universe. Mr. Muller, being a historian and not a pamphleteer, does not suggest that these differences are sharp and clear. Nevertheless, these differences are there, clearly there. East of that imaginary line referred to above, men looked upon the gods as all powerful and extremely capricious. They could be appealed to by mystic incantations and unreasonable sacrifices. The priesthood was the strongest single element in the community because they knew the "secrets" of appeasement of the gods. The basic thought was that the gods controlled everything and man was helpless.

It was some years later that a change in this attitude began

to appear. Largely centered on the Western coast of Asia
Minor, the Hellenes began to say that the gods were powerful but not absolutely so. They made mistakes; they had
weaknesses. So a man could struggle against them and oc-
casionally outwit them. In other words, though man was
weak and in need of help from the gods, he was also in some
measure in control of his own destiny. From this dramatic
change of attitude on the part of the Hellenes, the Greek
philosophy of political freedom was evolved. "If the gods
were not all-powerful, why then should a King be considered
so?"

From this beginning came the city state and the seed-bed
of the philosophies of Socrates, Plato and Aristotle. When,
under the leadership of the Jews, there developed the concept of one God, which concept ultimately gave us the Christian idea of man's free will under God, the pattern had
diverged still further from the old paths. Ultimately Christianity interacted with the Greek idea, producing the belief
that each individual man, no matter how lowly of estate,
had a dignity and a worth that was sacred. This degree of
value placed upon the individual caused men to believe
that man therefore had some measure of control over his
own destiny.

It must be noted here that this development of attitudes
never has prevailed in the East. The spread of Communism
today has shown the classic symptoms of having been influenced by the concept mentioned above as characteristic
of the people east of the imaginary line. "Man is nothing—
the gods are all powerful—we need a priesthood to intercede
for us." Since every action has a reaction, the fatalistic

East is reacting via Communism. For Communism utterly rejects the theory that the East has held to so long, i.e., man is a cipher in the predestined order of things.

It says man is everything and he is in complete control of his destiny. The logical next step is to reject the idea of a supreme being. The state is supreme and the people are the state. Since the word "freedom" does not arouse great emotions in the breast of the Easterner, he cannot revolt against that which he does not instinctively hate—authoritarianism. "East is East and West is West and never the twain shall meet" was more than a poetical analysis of the situation. It was actually true. Thus the Westerner found himself frustrated considerably when he tried to interpret the upheavals and national aspirations of the East in the light of his frame of reference alone. The minds of the people of the East did not work in the same framework as those whose spiritual ancestors were the Hellenes. At least they have not done so in the past. There is every evidence that Communism may change that attitude at last. And, alas, the change will not be for the best. Either for the Easterner or the Westerner.

Now let us return to our main theme, the amazing advance of Christianity. Though no one can be sure, it is probable at one time in those first centuries that Christians outnumbered any other single religious group. If so, then it did not hold true for long. Mohammedanism was soon to challenge Christianity. The challenge was actually carried to Western soil. The prospects of victory were frightening. The methods of Islamic "conversion" were even more frightening. What there was in the Islamic faith that appealed so highly to the Easterner, was appalling to the man of the West. And mustering every force available, the West actually fought for its life. At the Battle of Tours in 732, the tide was turned and the Moslem was turned back. The Northern Coast of Africa was from that time on lost to the Christian sphere of influence and remains lost to it today.

It was in the period immediately preceding and following this invasion that Christianity began to lose its forward thrust. Not because it had been defeated and crushed. Not because it had been superseded by something better. Not because it no longer had an appeal to the downtrodden and the oppressed. It had all the old elements of power. But its followers had committed the one sin that the Christian philosophy will not permit. They had forgotten the call to world advance through mission activity. This is the cardinal crime against the spirit of Christianity. When the thrust forward ceases, the drift backward begins. Success always breeds success and likewise with failure.

When the success story of Christianity's spread was blunted, its followers began to grow cold. Ecclesiasticism and desire for power took the place of the simple heart-throb of one man for another. The ugly years of shame that we call the Dark Ages came in on the wings of a dull-minded laity and a careless clergy. "Conversions" were accomplished through Church-State marriages of abomination and spiritual-secular relationships of adultery. The Church of those unhappy centuries was rich and proud and sinful. It had moved from the position of the aggressor to the defender of the status quo. We will have more to say about this. Suffice to say, that this, more than any other single item, is accountable for the many shortcomings found in the chapters of the later life of the Christian movement.

The world's most feared idea had not been defeated, proven wrong or outgrown. It was just forgotten for the time being.

THREE

The Flame Flickers

As WE HAVE ALREADY ESTABLISHED, IT IS COMMON KNOWLEDGE that Christianity had its dark ages. But these dark chapters did not come as a result of a flaw in the Gospel. They did not occur because it was discovered that by preaching a Gospel with repentance of sin and the forgiveness of God in it, men were not really changed. For there is no instance in Christian history where when the message of Christianity came to grips with pagan religions or materialistic philosophies it did not succeed eminently. When the Apostle Paul met the Greek mind, with all its intellectual power, in open and fair conflict, it became the "power of God unto salvation, to the Jew first and also to the Greek." Paul's experience as he faced the intellectual snobs of Athens is a case in point. Every word he spoke struck at some counter-belief of his hearers. And the day arrived when the Acropolis and the Areopagus fell into ruin, while the faith Paul preached became recognized as the hope of the world.

No, Christianity did not suffer its defeats at the hands of some superior idea. It went into decline in those middle ages for the same reasons it suffers today. And it can recover its virility in the same manner as it did in the Reformation

—by having a burning concern for human need and human values in the light of Divine intention.

This burning concern seems to have risen and fallen in direct ratio to the value Christians placed upon their acquired status in the society in which they lived. Strangely enough, it appears to work something like this: as the Christian Church has developed in its capacity to do something big, the less it has been willing to use that capacity. In other words, the less we Christians have had to risk, the more willing we have been to accept risk. When we trade the goal, "win the world to Christ," for the goal, "peace of mind," the role of the Christian aggressor grows increasingly less attractive. And whenever the Christian forces of the world have committed this "sin of Esau," they have not only suffered immeasurably themselves, but the world that looked to them for spiritual leavening has invariably suffered great spiritual apostasy. In the opinion of many, we have been in one of these dreaded phases of Christian drifting for the past half-century or longer.

But other instances of the same thing can be traced back to the beginning of Christian history. When we seek to account for this recession of spiritual power on the part of Christianity, three reasons stand out. For the sake of dramatization, let us call them:

1. The Gospel According to Blur
2. Double Exposure Church Members
3. Over-Stuffed Churches

The Gospel According to Blur made its first appearance soon after the master teacher began His divine work. It simply amounted to confusing the teachings of Christ to such an extent that men could no longer discern what He said from what someone thought He said. One of the first great controversies in the church came over a misunderstanding of the doctrine of salvation. When is a man saved? How is a man saved? What can a man do to save himself? Did salvation consist of Christ plus something else? Despite the clear statements concerning the adequacy of faith alone, someone began to cloud the issue with the idea of faith plus works, or faith plus church membership, or faith plus a vow of poverty, or faith plus self-inflicted humiliating punishment. Since the New Testament as we know it had not been compiled, these self-styled interpreters had a field day.

So the foundations were laid for a group who preached a blurred Gospel. And when the vision which Christ brought began to lose its clarity, it lost its ability to challenge as well.

When those among the Christian forces lost their zeal, the world tended immediately to classify Christianity as "just another religion." A new "Pantheon" was created in which Christianity sat like an idol in its own little niche. Side by side with the other world religions, its hucksters called out, "Step right up, folks, lay down your money and take your choice; everybody gets a prize!" This was a far, far cry from what Peter had meant when he said, "There is none other name under heaven given among men, whereby we must be saved."

The very well-springs of Christian belief were thus poisoned. The consequences were disastrous. The splinter-effect was the first sign of decline to appear. Innovations on the Christian theme became the order of the day. Some say it began with the death of Simeon, the last of the grand old men who had known Jesus and the twelve disciples, in A.D.

111. A writer in 1531, by the name of Sebastian Franck, wrote that the alteration of "the outward Church of Christ" took place "right after the death of the Apostles," or approximately A.D. 131 (A Letter to John Campanus, SAW). Later writers of the radical school set the fall or corruption of the Church during the era of Constantine when the union of Church and State was forged.

But the "when" of this "spiritual adultery" on the part of the Church is not the concern of this book. It is the "fact" of this condition that is of importance to us at this moment. Christianity, "the world's most feared idea," had at last been brought to heel with all of its mighty forces for change and regeneration stripped from it; the poor wretched thing crawled away to occupy some ornate temple or some classical Cathedral and surrounded by the trapping of silver and gold and the mumbo-jumbo of a priesthood, it had lost its sense of divine mission and revolutionary power. There is little doubt on the part of any group of thinking men that were the simple man of Galilee to return today, He would not recognize, for the most part, the Church He "loved and gave Himself for." Dressed in its finery and rolling in its riches, it parades down the streets of the world with pomp and circumstance; and He who gave Himself for us would have to stand on the side line and weep in shame. "Therefore I tell you, do not be anxious about your life, what you shall eat or what you shall drink, nor about your body, what you shall put on. . . . Your heavenly father knows that you need them all" (Matthew 6:25 and 32, RSV). But this, like so many of the simple lessons He taught, had received the "blur treatment."

So the Church of Christ which had been carefully identi-

fied with meeting human need and answering the requirements of the spirit of man had been removed from its original
frame and had been identified with riches and political
power. To the millions of men in this world who could not
read, much less understand the religio-political aspects of
the so-called Christian Church, this resulted in paganism
or worse. The original attempt of Satan, however, was
not the blur treatment. His original attempt was to stamp
out Christianity by force as was pointed out previously.
These persecutions began under Nero about the time of the
martyrdom of Paul and continued intermittently for centuries. Wherever the early Christians appeared they were
subjected to indignities beyond description. . . . "Destitute,
afflicted, ill-treated . . . wandering over deserts and mountains, and in dens and caves of the earth" (Hebrews 11:37–
38, RSV).

But the loss of earthly comforts could not force these
people to give up their faith in Christ. Thus violence failed.
By defeat the people conquered and as thousands were imprisoned and slain, other thousands arose to take their place.
So a new plan was devised. The adversary now endeavored
to accomplish by artifice what he had failed to gain by
force. The resulting alliance between idolatry and Christianity proved to be far more successful than any persecution
had ever been. Thus the early faith was placed in real
peril for the first time. Satan had insinuated himself into the
Church by a program of modification and compromise and
had succeeded in corrupting the clean, clear waters of faith
in Christ until they became murky and clouded with decep-
tion and false teaching. It became impossible for a majority
of the believers to discern between sacerdotalism and genu-

ine Christian doctrine, New Testament style. After a long and severe conflict, the remaining faithful believers determined to dissolve all union with the apostate Church. They saw that separation was an absolute necessity if they were to remain true to the word of God. From that day to this there has been a faithful minority who have been unwilling to pay the asking price for peace within Christendom at the expense of their fidelity to God. If unity could only be purchased by compromising truth and righteousness, then let there be disunion, no matter how disgraceful it may appear to a scoffing world.

But Satan's campaign of Blur went on. The nominal "conversion" of Constantine in the Fourth Century was the cause of great rejoicing among all who had been deluded by the Blur philosophy. The world, cloaked in the robes of pride and emperor-approval, walked in the front door of the apostate Church, and the program of corruption picked up its pace. Paganism became the conqueror and her evil spirit took control of the Christian movement.

The reading of the Bible was discouraged and only official interpretation of it was permitted. Thus the true teachings of the scripture received the blur treatment. From there they moved to the adoration of the saints including relics and images. Superstition and religious ignorance were promoted and encouraged in order to strengthen the hand of the prelates in power. Eventually the supremacy of the Church at Rome and its Bishop became the keystone of the world-wide program of these false leaders. When this was finally agreed to by a majority of the nations of the world, the "dark ages" of history descended upon the world.

Suppression supplanted liberty and tradition replaced the

word of God. A man had actually succeeded in establishing himself as the sole mediator between God and other men, and was therefore implicitly obeyed. As the centuries have rolled by, men have attempted from time to time to throw off and even overthrow this power. The history of their success is written around the names of Wycliffe, Martin Luther, Zwingli and others. The price they had to pay was often the supreme one. But they proved that the flame that was appearing to flicker before going out entirely, was actually to continue to burn by the grace of God and the faith of His faithful followers.

This is not to indicate that the method and original intent of Satan have changed. They have not. There is not a major, nor, in fact, a minor doctrine of the New Testament faith which has not been rearranged, deliberately misinterpreted, watered down or blurred by the unthinking or the deliberate agents of compromise. The campaign and the results are witnessed on every hand.

The immediate and present-day results of the blur treatment is the over-stuffed church of today. Not in numbers primarily, for this may or may not be an evil. But we speak now of one of the most serious ailments of modern Christianity, spiritual indigestion. The swallowing, or attempt to swallow, of the unregenerated church member has proved to be the culmination of the blurring of the requirements of true Christian conversion.

Horizontal expansion has always been a prime program of Christianity. That seems to have been Paul's concept of his calling as an apostle to the Gentiles. Going out under the sponsorship of the early Church and under the leadership of the Holy Spirit, he did not stay in one place longer than two years (Ephesus). His constant roaming of the Roman world sowed the seed of the Gospel and resulted in indigenous churches almost everywhere he went. This was as it should be and it received the blessing of God. But the enthusiasm of the latter-day would-be Pauls has brought us to the present-day state of colossalism versus spiritual purity. As a result, there is actually reason to believe that the vast numbers who make up the Christian churches of today have less impact upon modern life than did the mere handful that propagated the faith in the first centuries after Christ. Why?

The Church of Christ has always found itself engaged in two programs. The winning of the lost to a saving knowledge of Christ and the growing of those won into mature Christian warriors. The New Testament, and particularly the teachings of Jesus, have little to say about the winning of lost men. Apparently it was taken for granted that saved men would tell others.

Look at the writings of Paul. Every one of them was written to the saved. All of them are filled with various and sundry admonitions to the new Christian and their leaders as to the way and means to grow in grace and in knowledge of the Lord Jesus Christ. But we cannot be led by the *lack* of information on the actual winning of men. Both elements are absolutely essential to the growth and spread of the Gospel. Now, as long as these two elements stay in balance, the program of expansion is true to the word, whether the program be in a small church or a large. However, the moment the desired horizontal expansion supersedes the building of mature Christians, then trouble moves in. This is undoubtedly the reason the ministry of Christ and his disciples seemed to "major" on the perfecting of the faith of the saved.

Many of the most ridiculous spectacles of the past history of Christendom have resulted from rank distortions of the desire for growth numerically. History tells of armies being "baptized" by marching them into a river and of the priests standing in a body of water with the branch of a tree in hand, with which they were able to swish through the water and into the air over ranks of people or soldiers who marched past, thus "baptizing them into the faith." Though we do not stoop to such foolish methods today, yet the spirit of these practices are with us today. As one man put it, "The stork is the world's greatest missionary."

What has been the result? The answer is obvious. The spiritual temperature of the present-day church has been lowered to the point when the world can easily ignore a body of people who make no more impression on society than most churches make today. Over-stuffed, the churches are being overrun. Consider, for instance, careful admission of men and women into the Communist party, even in Russia, where the actual Communist party consists of no more than nine million people, in a nation of 208 million people. But, in spite of their small number, their dedication to their cause makes their influence felt on the one and three-quarter billion people in the world today. Sheer number is not the answer, if it is no more than number for number's sake. This forms the burden of embarrassment of American Christian missionaries around the world today. Faced with the problem of their own so-called "Christian" nation possessing the high crime wave and high divorce rate, they are torn between extending the reach of the Gospel by way of new converts and new churches or "majoring" on the growth of mature Christians who will make a real impact on their own community and nation. Actually they have no choice in the matter. The Gospel seed travels with the spiritual winds of the world. Despite what the world believes, great Christians of New Testament zeal are being grown in great numbers all over our world. In front of and behind the iron and bamboo curtains the age-old miracle of re-birth is taking place. And everytime it happens the Gospel's power to change men is proved anew. It works! It still works! Our problem is to see that its power has worked in the heart of every member received into our churches. Without that, the flame will flicker and die.

Almost every one of us has had the misfortune of failing to turn the film in our camera after taking a picture. Then when we snap the next shot, and receive the print from the developer we see the resultant "double exposure." As disheartening as it is on film, it is ten times more so in the image of the Christian to the eyes of the world. What does the true Christian really look like? What does he really believe? What does he really stand for? Actually, we have produced an image that has no meaning because it has no relation to reality.

Which "Christian" did the Gospel produce, the one who believes as a Baptist or the one who believes as an Episcopalian? Their images vary considerably to the outsider. Never mind the fact that in either case, if true conversion took place, the position on the essentials is the same. The truth is that to the man in the street, we have failed to provide him with a good picture showing the results of conversion. A "before" and "after" portrait is missing in far too many cases. Make no mistake now as to what is being discussed. We know that Christians are not stamped out with "cookie cutters." But that does not mean that the world does not have a perfect right to say, "If you are followers of Christ, then act like it. We can read what He was like, but we can't quite tell whether you are like Him or not."

Our day and generation is going to be forced to take sides one way or the other. The threat of Communism will see to that. The fantastic expansion of Communism can be blunted with a similarly fantastic growth in Christian example as well as numbers. The world must be shown what a true Christian is and how he reacts to the critical problems that face us. To do any less is to assure our defeat in this battle for existence. The true reflection of the truly converted growing Christian is an essential part of the anatomy of survival in our day.

Though there have been many, many tendencies toward decline and resultant weaknesses growing out of the above described internal shortcomings, the principal and most apparent has been the loss of the spirit of militancy which characterized the early church. When and if these weaknesses are corrected (and many evidences appear on every hand that they may be), then the thrust forward of Christianity will again be witnessed by our world. Make no mistake, the power is still there. The Holy Spirit still moves among the people of God. The concern of Christians today must be to understand the call to world conquest as issued by the Saviour when He commanded us to "Go into all the world and make disciples" and to understand the leading of the Holy Spirit toward the fulfillment of this command. The need for speed and urgency is being dramatized before our very eyes in the emergence of new strength among the animistic religions of Africa and the sudden spurt of growth of Mohammedanism, Buddhism and Hinduism. But this will be dealt with later. In the meantime, the forces of "preparing to win the world" are still in command of most mission efforts of Christian denominations. They've been "preparing" for generations, even centuries. And the preparation has seldom, if ever, "paid off" in the kind of success that the disciples of Jesus experienced when they made their supreme effort. To be true, "ploughing precedes reaping" and "a strong home front is essential to a strong battle front." But each is a part of the key to success. To become preoccupied with laying ground work on which to build later can be and may already be the great sin of modern mission efforts.

If someone were to find fault with the above insistence to "launch out" now, let him be reminded that for all intents and purposes we are living in very nearly the same kind of world that Christianity came into so many centuries ago. Language, world tensions, communication possibilities and nationalistic goals make the situation so similar it is almost uncanny. The major difference is that the disciples of Jesus lived and died by the commandment, "Go ye." It was the rediscovery of the real meaning of this command that propelled William Carey into his modern mission movement. When we can come to the place where the command becomes personal with us, then we too will live and die by its force. Gradualism as a means of winning the world to Christ has been Satan's curse on our mission efforts. And every time conservative leadership has taken over the reins of this great supernaturally commanded and blessed ministry, it has ground to a painful halt or an imperceptible edging-forward, to say the most. Did Jesus really mean "on this rock I will build my church and the gates of hell shall not be able to withstand the onslaught"? If so, and He did, then it's high time some sort of "onslaught" be launched by God's people. It cannot be that He did not intend it . . . it can only be that we are not ready and willing to move out on faith. We sing, "Like a mighty army moves the Church of God," when nothing could be less true of the thrust of God's people today.

FOUR

Let Christianity Meet the World's Second Most Feared Idea

FEW THINKING AMERICANS WILL DENY THAT THE UNITED STATES has had only one policy in the field of foreign affairs since 1945. That policy is to restrict by force the expansionistic efforts of the Soviet Union. At first we had the sole possession of the nuclear power to act as a frame of reference for all our decisions and pronouncements. Acting on the premise that might in military matters would keep the world on its feet, we turned our backs—as a nation, mind you—on more vital human values.

Then something happened that our leaders should have foreseen. Russia exploded not only an atomic bomb but our "make the world safe through power" theory as well. For a time it was possible to reassess our national policy: to return to a more humane and more spiritual solution to the problems that faced the spirit of all mankind. Actually it was not so much "the problems" but "the Problem," human survival, that needed to be solved.

But even then there was no one with sufficient wisdom and moral leadership to step forward and sound a call to reason. Having committed our nation into the hands of the political, scientific and military authorities, we were being led down the one-way street of the threat of total annihilation of our enemies, as the only means to settle our problems. We have finally arrived on this fateful journey at the place where we cannot use or permit to be used the weapon system we have perfected, and we cannot conceal the fact that when that is removed from our arsenals of defense, we are bankrupt.

Now in the face of these indisputable facts, where do we go from here? First, we must admit that the situation is actually a moral debacle. It was arrived at by a series of steps that reach back into pre-war history:.

1. Political and military pigmies, wearing the boots of political giants, refused to clothe President Wilson with the strength he needed to commit our nation to an equal partnership in the international community and the responsibilities that would arise therefrom.

2. Moral and spiritual pigmies, wearing the boots of spiritual giants, refused to speak out in the halls of international justice when the first crimes of the post-World War I era were being committed.

3. A nation had as its chief preoccupation, during the 20's, the externals of piety, such as the Volstead Act, and had, as its chief amusement, the Catholic-baiting era of Al Smith.

With these deep fissures in the American spiritual landscape, the public lost faith in all its leaders; they elected a do-nothing president (Coolidge) and listened to a believe-nothing ministry and read the works of a nothing-sacred literati.

Now the end result of all of this was not the roaring twenties or the depression thirties, as you might expect. The results of fateful and incorrect decisions seldom if ever appear to the eye so dramatically or so soon. They generally lie under the surface and smolder for a number of years. And so it was with these strategic errors of moral and spiritual weakness.

Here is what happened. When the totalitarian powers goose-stepped onto the world scene and when they committed their atrocities against Ethiopia and Poland, they, in effect, announced to the world a return to the dimension of warfare not heard of since the days of Genghis-Khan-total-war with attacks on the unarmed masses of civilians. Thus, terrorism and population extermination became instruments of governments that frankly intended to rule this world. When this fact became apparent to the morally decent people of the world, they were shocked indescribably. Then, when the first effects of the horror wore off there were angry cries for retaliation, in kind, on these monsters.

Now was the time for some truly great leader to come to the forefront on the international councils. As things stood, a wise, prudent and spiritual voice could have convinced our part of the world that this behavior was that of a beast and that the way to fight him was not as another beast. Being made in God's image and believing in the power and presence of the living God, we must fight in a way other than bestial. But, alas, such was not the case. The great pulpits of America, one by one, lined up with those who recommended total war on the enemy. Writers, artists, molders of public opinion joined in and so it was that before the atomic bomb was even conceived, our nation and our Western Civilization joined in the complete acceptance of the Nazi and Fascist doctrine of total war, with a determination to exceed the efforts of our enemies in this field.

Obliteration bombing was the strategy used. The Americans by day, the English by night. And, with the almost complete agreement of our nations, we proceeded systematically to destroy entire cities and their population.

This was the historic beginning of the present-day situation, from which there seems to be no retreat. For, you observe, we adopted these means with what we considered to be a high purpose: survival! We operated no concentration camps with their horrible crematoriums but one fire-bomb raid on Tokyo burned 270,000 people to death in *one* night! And when we dropped our atom bombs on Hiroshima and Nagasaki, we reached the ultimate step from which there is no return. Oh, for a moment, there were cries of guilt and from some pulpits there were calls for national confession of sin against God and man. But this soon died out and we rationalized the matter by saying, "Millions of American lives were saved by ending the war so swiftly." That may be so, though it is debatable. But while we were saving lives, we lost our souls! We had, as a nation, abandoned moral and spiritual restraint as a part of our way of life. We had passed the signal to our leaders to proceed in the perfecting of a weapon based on the splitting of the atom.

We have stood by quietly as explosion after explosion has fouled the atmosphere of the world and we have had only a handful of national leaders to appeal to us on the basis of the moral and spiritual issues concerned to cease this wickedness and, in the interest of the health of the children of the world, born and unborn, to stop this miserable crime against humanity.

If it were possible to point to actual proof of the effectiveness of this adoption of a policy completely foreign to Western Christian Civilization's code of honor, then perhaps some minute justification might be acceptable. But this is not the case. Czechoslovakia, Poland and Korea are cases in point where nuclear power politics meant nothing. The Communists rolled along while we held our "disaster raid" drills in our schools and rattled our bombs to try to stop them. They know, as our leaders must know, that in the field of human degradation and physical slavery and death, they are fighting their kind of war on their chosen battlefields, when and as they please. We could not start a war, preventative or aggressive—our people would not stand for it. So, all dressed up in our H-bomb clothes, we have absolutely nowhere to go. We have been neatly driven into a cul-de-sac in the realm of a war of violence. Our leaders and our people chose a road we cannot walk, a role we cannot play and an attitude we cannot defend.

The answer must be a new road, a new role and a new attitude, and this time they must be based on the moral and spiritual battlefields of human dignity and spiritual farsightedness. This change in character does not mean a surrender to Russian Communism. It does not mean laying down our arms and turning our cheek to be slapped. Those who see this as the only alternative are the very ones who have helped bring about this present condition. Nor do the threats to our survival increase. There is only one step now between survival and obliteration anyway and the possibility of someone taking that step accidentally is such a spectre that there are some men who can hardly sleep at night. No matter how hard a man may try, he cannot convince all of us that there are only two positions: atomic retaliation or total surrender.

There is a third position, represented by the resurgence of dynamic moral leadership, that says there is a way out that is honorable, that will extend the necessary assurances of freedom to the nations of the world and at the same time, reverse the direction of the moral and spiritual life of our world. The possibility lies in the direction of a bold approach to the Commission—the Great Commission given to us by Christ. "Go therefore and make disciples of all nations, baptizing them in the name of the Father and of the Son and of the Holy Spirit, teaching them to observe all that I have commanded you; and lo, I am with you always, to the close of the age" (Matthew 28:19-20, RSV). By thus choosing our own battleground, and our own weapons and fighting when and as we are taught, we once more resort to the kind of "war" we can win, and the kind that will rescue the nations of the world from the brink of disaster. And we leave those who prove themselves to be the enemies of mankind to be policed and jailed as international criminals, as any decent community in the world does to maintain order. No one can deny that there is a hoodlum element in the community of nations. And no one would deny the need to control and contain these nations. For this purpose, guns and planes and tanks and bombs must be maintained and be as ready for use as the police sergeant's pistol.

But this is a far different outlook on world problems from

the one we have today. For as of this moment, we are guilty of forgetting the things that set us apart from all those in every generation of man who forget God and operate on the basis of the builders of the tower of Babel; we are forgetful of a moral and spiritual intelligence derived from the worship of that God, Jehovah.

When the factor of spiritualized intelligence re-enters the field of combat, human desire will produce the imaginative proposals that will bring our world about and begin building a merciful society based on the teachings of Christ. While common sense tells us we must not minimize nor oversimplify the tremendous problems to be faced and solved, this one thing we know: if there is a God, and there is, we will be walking more closely to His will, and with this sense of mission and divine approval, neither Russia nor any other robber-nation will be able to stand up against the impact this will make on the world. If the charge against these ideas is "oversimplified optimism," please reserve judgment for a later moment.

Instead of recommending the kind of liberal optimism that usually arises from a soft heart and perhaps a soft head, this book proposes the hopeful belief that man still possesses a free will and is therefore capable of saving himself as a result of relating himself properly to God and thus finding the idea or ideas which will help him shape his future in a way that is pleasing to his Creator. The basis for this hope makes sense if we look at the world as a place where we can discover that causes can be defined and that results can be predicted. Our generation needs to be reminded that we are not living in a madhouse on the midway of some circus where anything can happen but nothing can be explained.

Regardless of what Marx or Spengler or any of the old dark gods of the Northern European forest may have said, we still have the power of choosing. Our world may still be redeemed with the power of an idea from God. The thing for us to remember is that a bad idea is just as explosive or powerful as a good idea.

Ideas are bombs, and sometimes when they land in the mind of a man who is an evil genius, they result in world-wide spasms and convulsions of pain and sorrow and bloodshed. But when they land again in the heart of a good man, with the same energies to spare and willingness to sacrifice himself if necessary, in order to share this idea with the world, then no price is too great for him to pay. It was Colonel Nasser, the present leader of the United Arab league, who said, when speaking of the organization of Arab peoples of the world, "I found a cause looking for a man." This same thing has happened many times in history. I am convinced it has happened in our day and time.

There is a cause—the cause of world missions on a massive and gigantic basis. This cause is looking for some man or group of men who will be willing to pay the price so that Christian forces of our world may be united in a way by which we may march out to meet the needs of our world and to accept the challenge thrown by atheistic Communism. This cause is roaming the world today looking for men to pick it up, assume it and be willing to lay down their lives, if necessary, to see that it succeeds.

What is this cause of which we speak? Let me try to formulate it. It is based upon the premise that our world is more than half-pagan and that the pagan part of the world is rising up to challenge the Christian part of the world. This pagan part of the world has so much in its favor, including strength, numbers and satanic wisdom that there are millions upon millions of people in the world who are beyond hope. At the present moment, there is no organization or group of organizations involved in world missions that has the slightest possible chance of succeeding on a massive scale. No denomination or group of denominations is properly organized to reach this world for Christ. This sweeping statement includes the World Council of Churches, the National Council of Churches and the Roman Catholic Church. In the present set of circumstances, there is not an effort being made in our world today that is worthy to be called a World Mission program. Now we have reached the place in the course of human affairs when the individual "empires," so to speak, of the various denominations, and the political aspirations and ambitions of Councils of Churches, should be subordinated to the desperation which fills our world. This desperation is comparable to the desperation which Britain felt when Germany fell upon her with air power and the threats of invasion.

That's where our world stands today. And for the sake of changing the course of history, accepting the challenge of Satan embodied in international Communism, the church bodies of the world need to form some sort of Council, without organic union, where they can sit down, coordinate their efforts and share with one another information. Working side by side, they would excite the enthusiasm and the imagination of the Christian world, and bring about a spirit of real sacrifice in giving. We must accept the challenge that God is evidently holding out to us when He calls more and more people to World Missions. We must accept this challenge and meet it on a massive scale. I believe that this simple idea, properly enlarged, designed, coordinated and oriented to our world, can change the face of history in our day and for the foreseeable future of our world .

The people of our world are as needy as they have ever been, but they have more passion and more desire to improve their lot and to find a better way to live than they have ever had before. Yet in the face of this, no major denomination has more than 1500 to 2000 missionaries scattered over two and a half billion people on the face of this earth. Moreover, all the missionaries combined, of the Protestant denominations, number only a few thousand. The thinking people of the world can draw only one conclusion, and that is that the Christian Churches of America and of Western Civilization have never made a serious effort to win the world to Christ. This is either because they do not believe it can be done or they think that Christianity is incapable of challenging the philosophies of other portions of the world. Or is it that we do .not believe in Christianity enough to be willing to make the effort?

Surely it must be one of the first two suppositions. It cannot be that it is the last, "We do not believe enough." In no event will our task be easy. In our kind of world it will be exceedingly difficult.

A world of relative values and diluted rationalism will never be able to stand against a world of absolute values and headlong emotion. Power and tyranny add up to being nothing more than absolute values. They tend to produce great strength of will. The fact that they are powers of Satan does not diminish their force at all. It only means that they are uncreative and that in their triumph, they can do nothing but destroy. It is common knowledge among students of history that the power of an idea may be multiplied and squared to the nth degree through the taste of a little power. Once the walls of civilization have been breached, the strength of the enemy seems to grow because his expectations grow and he is tasting the pleasure of success. So it was when the Germans proved that they were victorious. The Italians joined in, feeling that if Germany could do it, they could do it also. With the spread of this explosive idea of tyranny among nations, the Japanese jumped into the fray. To us it was like a dream as we sat back and watched the world being destroyed by the cruelty and power-hunger of people to whom only a few short months or years before, we had referred as our friends. And now, with justice and kindness completely expunged from their nature, they operated crematoriums in which they burned men and women; evil with them reached a degree almost beyond discussion. In the meantime, cherishing our way of life, we seemed temporarily unable to match their will power with our will power, and we stood on the brink of destruction.

It should be remembered that Hitler himself wrote that passions which he intended to inspire would have to be met and conquered with an opposite passion and not with merely a force. He indicated in *Mein Kampf* that the revolution he intended to bring about would not be beaten as a result of superior armies or navies. Instead, it would be beaten only as a result of someone bringing against him an explosive idea of greater power. It is common knowledge that Hitler knew that what he was about to let loose on our world was nothing more than a deluge of barbarians. In short, he was turning the clock of history back to the days of Genghis Khan or before, where total war was made by tribe against tribe, people against people, and soldiers and civilians alike fell under the sword of the conqueror. Hitler's instinct told him that there was no one left on earth who believed enough in a great idea, in an idea great enough to tower over and thus destroy his own superman concept of the Aryan race. We all lived through a breathless era from 1933 or 1934 down to the beginning of the battle of Britain where none of us was quite sure there was an idea left in the world strong enough to oppose him. The truth of the matter is that the idea of power and tyranny has always had great appeal to the dark places of the human heart. This appeal had managed to loose energies and desires and passions that had been held in check so long that it was almost possible to believe that they didn't exist. However, when the suggestion of expansion and unlimited booty was offered to a nation, meaning Germany, of course, that nation turned loose such reserves of energy that it almost conquered the world. The truth is also that no one with a lukewarm faith could stand against an explosive idea such as Hitler had, and the same thing is true today.

If one is to understand this, one must learn a good deal about Communism itself. In order to understand the power of the idea of Communism, we need to set down, as briefly as possible, the concept of Communism and something of the reason why it has captured the imagination of so many millions of people. The basic object of Marxism is to plan distribution of the world's wealth among its human inhabitants. This idea of the distribution of wealth did not originate with Karl Marx. It actually originated with the famous English economist of the nineteenth century, John Stuart Mill, who taught that the production of goods came about as a result of the province of natural economic laws. He also taught that the responsibility of distributing the wealth that arose as a result of the production of goods, came under the province of man-made laws. Marx carried Mill's basic idea to a great extreme. He was convinced that the unequal distribution of the products of labor under capitalism actually arose from the economic philosophy that each individual had the right to hold and possess and use for his own purpose the fruits of his own labor. Thus, he had the power to accumulate savings for his own subsequent use. This then became his "capital." In the light of this definition, Marx said that the generally accepted capitalistic concept of a man having the right to the fruits of his labor was unfair and unjust. Therefore it had to be discarded. In its place he put the idea that man was not really born with any natural rights; whatever rights he actually had, came to him as a result of the State in which he lived; therefore, Marx believed that the product of the man's labor belonged to the State in which he resided.

If therefore man had no inherent rights, according to orthodox Communism, then he had no right to the product of his own labor. As a natural consequence of this line of thinking, the Communist idea is that the State has the right to gather together the fruits of everyone's labor and hold this collected wealth for whatever use might be necessary in order for the State to carry on its various social, economic and government functions. It assumed that it had more power and more wisdom in the proper distribution of what it held on a just and equitable basis among the people who made up the State. It amounted to this: everyone pitched in with all he had, let the government collect the material results of his labor, either physical or mental, and then each man in turn periodically received from the Government a sum which the Government deemed to be fair and equitable.

Now this thought, of course, is fascinating. So fascinating, in fact, that it has caught the imagination of millions. And the bare idea is, of course, quite simple. All that remained to be done was for someone to work out the details. In other words, what is a fair basis of distribution to the individual? This, of course, has been the built-in booby trap in the present-day idea of Communism. There have been so many differences of opinion over what is a fair or workable distribution. In a recent discussion with confirmed Communists in the governmental realm, in Moscow, the writer was faced with the suggestion that Communism was first practiced by the early Christians and one individual referred to the distribution of food and wealth which occurred soon after the death of Christ and principally to the operation of the Christian Church in Jerusalem. In order to understand the difference between the communism of Biblical times and Communism today, certain facts must be brought out.

First, let me present certain facts on proposals for distribution of wealth and goods under present-day Communism. There are three outstanding proposals which have been used at various times and which may be used in various ways again.

The first proposal is that distribution must be in accordance with the true value of the services rendered by the individual.

The second is that distribution must be on the basis of each individual's needs, regardless of the value of the services which he renders to the State.

And the third is that the distribution of goods of equal value must be shared by all regardless of the value of the services rendered by the individuals to the State. Each individual is to receive goods according to his own choice.

The first proposal, to distribute according to the true value of services rendered by each person, while it seems just, would be impossible to administer. It would involve problems of such complexity and would result in so many injustices that it would prove to be unusable—in fact, it has so been proven.

The second proposal immediately brings to the surface the obvious difficulty of determining the reasonable needs of the individual. For there is an infinite variety of needs and there is the matter of the variability of each person's needs from time to time and from circumstance to circumstance. These difficulties alone make it utterly impossible to employ the proposed standard of the division of goods or wealth.

The third proposal is equally impossible. It assumes that one can first arrive at the net value for governmental needs. Secondly, it assumes that the balance can be divided among the people in the form of some sort of credit so that each individual can draw against these credits in order to meet his needs regardless of whatever services he may have rendered to the State. Keeping these things in mind, let us now look at the communism which was used in the early Christian Church in Jerusalem.

The first Church consisted at that time of a group of people bound together by excitement and desire, and committed to living day by day according to the truths which they had received from the teachings of Christ. These truths seemed now to be embodied in the lives of the Apostles who were with Him and who were now leading the early Church, since He was no longer among them in physical form. These first Christians felt impelled to remain together. They adhered steadfastly to this fellowship with a great sense of belonging together. This sense of belonging expressed itself not only in a common meal which they shared together, two, three or four times daily, but also in their prayers for one another and in their eagerness to provide for each other's needs. Listen to this passage, "And all who believed were together and had all things in common; and they sold their possessions and goods and distributed them to all, as any had need" (Acts 2:44–45, RSV). Now, as we said, some have seen in this an early instance of Communism. But the person who is familiar with the Bible will recall immediately the case of Ananias and Sapphira (Acts 5:1–11). A very cursory study of this case will show that no one was compelled to give to another. If this spontaneous generosity be communism, then it was a communism that differed from all other kinds of communism, and can only be properly described as a communism based upon religious love. It was a communism composed chiefly of those who consumed and a communism based upon the assumption that each of its members would continue to earn his living by whatever means of private enterprise suited him best. Note that he was taught to practice Christian generosity and Christian sacrifice with the fruit of his labor from his own field of private enterprise.

There is absolutely no evidence that there was any kind of organization along business lines whereby a group of these men or women joined together as producers in order to meet the need of the consumers. In the light of present-day society, communism is too formal a word to describe the spontaneous generosity of these early Christians. They had a new-found faith, and the joy which they received from this faith caused them to want to share, not to hoard, their possessions. This did not arise out of any economic theory which any of them held; it was merely due to the unity of interest which they shared as a result of Christian fellowship. A fellowship which made them feel like a family, and as a family they met the needs of one another as best they could. One could not properly identify or define their attitude unless he took into consideration their hope and belief that there would be a speedy return of Christ to this earth and that as a consequence, worldly possessions were of little or no value except as they perhaps shared in order to provide for the needs of the poor until Jesus came again. If this be communism, then its later state of having been abandoned by the saints of Jerusalem and elsewhere may be a pointer to present-day Communism and a warning as well.

As the persecution broke out against the Christians at Jerusalem, they were scattered in all directions. It was because of them that we have the record of Paul the Apostle, a man who engaged in the private enterprise of tent-making in order to meet his own needs, using those funds and other moneys which he collected to meet the needs of others, such as the Christians still remaining in Jerusalem. Their condition of poverty had been reported to him while on one of his missionary journeys.

With that out of the way, let us look at the eventual meeting of latter-day Christianity and present-day Communism. This meeting took place soon after the publication of the Communist Manifesto. The Communist Manifesto was written by Marx and Engels in 1848 and represents a declaration of war against capitalistic society. The Manifesto is international in its appeal. It speaks from the point of view that Capitalism is doomed to disappear and it calls upon laboring men of all countries to unite and "support every revolutionary movement in the existing social political order of Marx-Engels." Marx gave his movement the name "Communism" in order to keep his movement from being identified with what was popularly known then as Utopian Socialism.

When the Manifesto was first published, it caught the imagination of millions of workers all over the world. It contained great emotional appeal and it was written with an eloquence of language which was designed to catch their attention. For instance, listen to the closing statement, "The Communists disdain to conceal their views and aims. They openly declare that their ends can be attained only by the forcible overthrow of all existing social conditions. Let the ruling classes tremble at a Communist revolution. The proletarians have nothing to lose but their chains. They have a world to win. Working men of all countries, unite!"

The Manifesto first appeared in London, printed in the German language. It was later followed by publication in France just before the 1848 revolution. The first English translation appeared in London about 1850. Since then it has been published in almost all the languages of the world and distributed widely. The first portion of the Manifesto described the condition of the worker and presents a dismal picture of his future under Capitalism. He is described as being a part of Capitalistic Society which is designed to prevent the laborer from rising with the progress of industry; in fact, it is designed to bring it about that the laborer sinks deeper and deeper below the conditions of the existence of his own class. He will eventually become a pauper. While he is moving into pauperism, the ruling class will become more wealthy at his expense. Among the Manifesto's major proposals is, one, the abolition of private property; two, the elimination of the family as a social unit; three, the abolition of the exploitation of children by their parents; four, the elimination of the present system of marriage and the introduction of "an openly enterprise community of women" to effect the elimination of "prostitution, both public and private" and the abolition of "countries and nationalities" on the ground that working men have no country. This first section also recommends the discarding of the present systems of religion, philosophical thought and ideologies, because they have been outgrown and are no longer of value in the present social relations of our world.

The second section of the Manifesto has as its principal theme the wresting from the hands of the ruling class of all capital, all instruments of production and all productive forces, and concentrating them in the hands of the State. The Manifesto admits that this process will not be accomplished immediately. It states, "Of course, in the beginning, this cannot be effected except by means of despotic inroads on the rights of property and on the conditions of bourgeois production; by means of measures therefore, which appear economically insufficient and untenable, but which, in the course of the movement, outstrip themselves, necessitate further inroads into the existing social order, and are unavoidable as a means of entirely revolutionizing present modes of production." The second section also includes the abolition of the law and right of inheritance, confiscation of the property of all immigrants and rebels, the centralization of the means of communication, equal obligation of all to work and the combination of agriculture with manufacturing industries. Furthermore, it includes free education of all children in public schools and the abolition of child labor.

The third section of the Manifesto deals with matters of Communist literature and its final section is entitled "The Position of the Communist in Relation to the Various Existing Opposition Parties." It includes the above quoted famous call, invoking the unity of the workingmen of all countries. In the light of this exceedingly simplified outline of the Communist Manifesto, the average reader of the Bible can quickly compare with it the Sermon on the Mount, the Golden Rule and the teachings of Christ in the Gospels, which contain the Christian Manifesto, set down so that men can follow it. Both "ideologies" have been designed to change the face of the world. Each arrived in a similar period of history—a period when there was utter misery on the part of the great masses of people, when children were mistreated, and there was persecution and oppression on every hand, and corruption in government and brutality were everyday experiences. Thus brutalized and poverty-stricken, ground down and trod under by the ruling classes, the people of these similar periods received these marvelously different suggestions as to a way and means by which the average man could better his way of life. One served to relate man properly to the State. The other served to relate man properly to his Creator. Although Marx had many purposes in mind in the formulation and publication of the Communist Manifesto, one of his self-imposed tasks was the formidable one of presenting a solution to the so-called riddle of existence. He attempted not only to explain it but he also intended to give life a direction and a purpose. He sought to provide a substitute for religion and he did so by presenting what he regarded as a scientific explanation of the world and a rational explanation of man's place in this world.

Marx knew that in developing a philosophy of society, he had to formulate a hypothesis that had a dogmatic essence as its basis. If it had this dogmatic essence, then it must be accepted on faith in spite of its possible contradictions in scientific basis. It was necessary for him to find a way by which every event in history could be interpreted in accordance with his dogma. Then, if one challenged the dogma, he was challenging the way of life or the very basis of existence. This, of course, has resulted in the zigging and the zagging of his later followers. Their difficulties and their differences have caused many of them to deviate from the dogmatic hypothesis and to attempt to find a way whereby Communism could be actually practiced. It has resulted, as all of us know, in the twisting of the doctrine to fit whatever frame of reference is convenient.

Never has a national government stood so wretchedly naked and revealed in all its ugliness as in the process of "de-Goding" of Stalin. When one couples this revelation of the criminality of Stalin with the bloody crushing of the Hungarian revolt, one catches a glimpse of the enemy; sees him as he really is, capable of any crime. And what's worse, capable of twisting and turning as he seeks to meet circumstances by whatever means are necessary.

Lenin and Stalin began the task of making interpretations fit the circumstances of the hour, and these deviations have continued in a greater degree down to this present day. It is beyond the scope of this volume to delve deeply into these complicated deviations and changes. Suffice it to say that as the practical experience of Communism has entered into history, the concepts of mind, matter, ideas, forms, substance, idealism, materialism, all of these concepts have gone through change after change. The consequence of this twisting and turning is another revelation of the built-in booby trap in present-day Communism. For today we behold the spectacle of its leading theoreticians arranging and rearranging the philosophy of Communism to meet the changing circumstances of the world and thus often making themselves ridiculous in the eyes of their own party as they shift and turn, trying to meet each set of circumstances on the basis of expediency.

No student of foreign affairs vis-à-vis Russia will deny that this is a great weakness. It should be enough to blunt and break the Communistic thrust. It undoubtedly would be enough if the Western approach to the needy people of the world was different.

The gap between East and West is not a technological one. It is a psychological and spiritual gap. The key problem is not to supply economic techniques that are an improvement. In far too many cases this kind of assistance has actually aroused bitter resentment. "Change" is not desired or admired in the ancient East. The bringer of change is often despised. This is not difficult to understand if one sees the fragmentation of the organic Oriental Society under the impact of the West. If this revolution of methods is accepted, any socio-political ideals that may tend to accompany it are rejected. *Not because the ideals are abhorrent.* Russia presents ideals too. But because our economic assistance is always given through the existing government.

In the light of this fact, it is important to remember that economic progress in two-thirds of the world is in its inception. Whatever philosophic and strategic conditions exist at the time of the early phases of this progress will more than likely accompany it far into the future. These are the impressionable years among these people. And with whom do we work? The existing government which in many if not most of the instances is a symbol of corruption and oppression to the people. And with whom do the Russians work? The people themselves! From the bottom up, their policies are geared to the emotions of the people, while from the top down, our policy is predicated upon the maintenance of the existing order. How that problem can be solved is beyond the author. But one thing we know, the current "battle" for the uncommitted areas will not be solved to the safety and satisfaction of the West by the program described above. The "battle" will be won in the hearts of men who are willing to enter into a personal relationship with the man in the street in the needy two-thirds of the world and interpret to him in a sympathetic way how much we care and why. This cannot be done through "Point-Four" programs, or "economic missions" from our governments. Nor can it be done with a small handful of Christian missionaries working here and there, almost independently of one another, with no over-all plan that would to some extent insure relief and victory.

Someone is sure to ask, "Personal relationship? Are you recommending that thousands of Americans pack their bags and go overseas as missionaries? Is this possible, or wise?" Well, it may be both possible and wise. But at the moment it may appear to be neither. By personal relationship, we mean a relationship that is tangibly warm and Christian. A people-to-people program in the area of Christian brotherhood. The dedication of large sums of money, given through our churches, and the speeding-up of procurement and training programs for supplies and personnel. A quickening of activity on the part of God's people to be prepared to take part in and take advantage of the intellectual ideological bankruptcy of the Communist regions of the world. This process of bankruptcy is closer to being a reality than many realize. It is a fact that no major statement of Communist doctrine in Russia has taken place in more than thirty years.

The last one was Stalin's Foundations of Leninism. In the meantime, the Russian newspapers are full of activities calling attention to the shortcomings and inadequacies of the Communist totalitarian society. In a recent trip to Russia, the author was amazed at the news columns that were filled with biting criticisms of the Russian way of life.

FIVE

Communism's One Block
to Western Conquest

IN PRESENTING A GENERAL OUTLINE SUCH AS GIVEN IN THE
preceding chapter, one must be prepared to deal with the
objections and the attitude of the average Westerner. He
holds a certain attitude in regard to modern-day worldwide Christian mission efforts. He usually possesses one or
both of the following opinions.

1. "Missionaries are meddlers. If the people of a particular country have their own religion, we should
   leave them alone. To teach them to wear clothes or
   to read may create more problems than can be
   solved. After all, Christianity is not an international
   panacea. Its teachings may actually result in harm
   among certain people. Leave them as they are."
2. "I can't find any evidence to prove that Christianity
   has ever made a serious effort to win the world. Oh,
   there are records of mass baptisms and 'National
   Conversion' on the orders of a King or ruler. But as
   to reaching and winning men on a massive scale, no.

There never has been and never will be a really serious attempt to do this. Actually, to try to do so would be to try to make the ideals of Christianity do something they were not intended to do. This faith is a personal faith, and will always be held by a minority only. Of course, I have no objection to trying. Missionary work provides an outlet for the ladies' aid societies and for religious fanatics."

The fact is that nothing could please the Communists more than for all of us to adopt one or the other of these views. For if we do so, we shall remove the threat, the only threat, to their success that remains. That threat is an aroused Christian conscience rampant in the world. For the Communists of the world know, even if we don't, that the only thing that stands between them and eventual absolute world conquest is the Christian conscience, or the remnants of it, which still exist in the world.

If Christianity has played any important part in world affairs in these critical days, it has been here. For in the past five to ten years we have challenged them with money and fighting men almost every time they have sought to subjugate a nation which did not wish to be subjugated. Such action on our part has frustrated and maddened Communism more than once. Their anger may actually have been the cause of the Korean conflict in 1951. How? Let me relate the story this way:

For some time in the past, the Communist hierarchy has recognized the need for more information on what makes an American "tick." "Why," they have pondered, "will America be willing to go to war for the protection of the relatively

useless have-not nations five to ten thousand miles away
from their shores?" The answer to this question had to be
found, before another more important question could be
solved, "how can we find the source of this willingness?"
Consequently, let us assume, they determined to find a "laboratory" in which they could conduct some of the "live"
experiments (on living subjects) for which they are so famous. Being almost completely isolated from any danger
zone and being relatively valueless as real estate, yet easily
accessible to armies and supplies, Korea, for these and other
reasons, became their choice. A "fire" was deliberately started
there which obliged our nation eventually to meet them on
the battlefields and mountain tops of that unfortunate little
country. While this was taking place, special camps and
stockades were being prepared in a safe area behind Communist lines which would ultimately contain 7000 Americans
held as prisoners of war. This group of 7000 men was to be
the guinea pig in this "laboratory experiment" on the grand-
est of all scales.

Now let us look at these American "guinea pigs." The
average American soldier in a bunker on the front lines in
Korea expected that if he were captured by the Chinese
Communists he would be subjected to tortures often described by his World War II buddy back home.

He was sure that he would be subjected to some cruel
oriental atrocity such as having his fingernails pulled out.
Thus, when these men were captured, they afterward related, they were terrified by the possibilities of what lay
ahead.

Two or two and a half years later these men, or what remained of them, were released from this stockade and given

permission to return to their lines and ultimately to their homes in America. None of us need to be reminded of the shock and shame which we experienced when twenty-six of those men announced an intention to remain in Communist China the rest of their lives. They stated to news reporters and to our diplomats that they liked the Communist way of life and therefore never intended to return to America. "How can this be?" we asked ourselves and our neighbor. The defection aroused the Congress and the President. It was not only the about-face of these boys; there were also stories that indicated that other men in the camp had collaborated with the enemy and generally disgraced their uniform and their country. Some people claimed drugs had been used on our men. Others called it "brain washing," and indicated that a series of tortures had been used, which resulted in making moral "zombies" of our men.

Eventually the President directed that Major William E. Mayer, a psychiatrist in the U. S. Army, be sent to receive and interview at length all the men who did return. Major Mayer was to report his findings directly to the President. Thus, when the remaining four thousand men were released, approximately five hundred were directed to military hospitals in Tokyo where they were carefully questioned one at a time. Three months later William Mayer was flown to Washington to report to the President. His report was tape-recorded and classified. It was not released to the general public until some years later. When it was finally released, it was recognized that Major Mayer's studies and opinions did not necessarily represent the official attitude of our Government, nor were they necessarily absolutely correct. His observations, however, were based upon his unrestricted questioning of the first large cross-section of American youth who have ever been exposed for a period of time to Communist propaganda and Communist society. Major Mayer's questions and conclusions could possibly have been influenced by a captured document written by the Chief of Intelligence of the Chinese Peoples Volunteers in North Korea to the Chief of Intelligence of the Chinese Peoples Republic in Peiping. The original message, says Major Mayer, was titled "An Evaluation of the American Soldier." If this is true, and we have no reason to doubt it, it is my hypothesis that we captured a document containing the information for which the Communists started the Korean War.

"What makes an American tick? What will it take to separate him from his natural instinct to fight for the under-dog, to take the little fellow's part in any battle? Until we know the answer to that, we cannot overcome him in world affairs short of war. If we do find the answer, the world is ours!"

Here's what the document said:

"Based upon our observation of the American soldiers and their officers captured in this war for the liberation of Korea from the capitalist-imperialist aggression, some facts are evident. The American soldier has weak loyal-ties—to his family, his community, his country, his religion, and to his fellow soldier. His concept of right and wrong is hazy. He is basically materialistic, and he is an opportunist. By himself he feels insecure and frightened. He underestimates his own work and his strength and his ability to survive. He is ignorant of social values, social conflicts and tensions. There is little or no knowledge or understanding even among American university graduates of U. S. political history and philosophy; the federal, state and community organizations; states' and civil rights, freedom's safeguards; and how these allegedly operate within his own decadent system.

"He is exceedingly insular and provincial with little or no idea of the problems and the aims of what he contemptuously described as foreigners and their countries. He has an unrealistic concept of America's eternal and inherent, rather than earned or proven, superiority and absolute military invincibility. He fails to appreciate the meaning of and the necessity for military organization or any form of discipline. Most often he appears to feel that his military service is a hateful, unavoidable servitude to be tolerated as briefly as possible and then escaped from as rapidly as possible or he is what they themselves call a 'peacetime soldier' who sees it only as a soft and a safe job. Both of these types resent hardship and sacrifice of any description as if these things were unreasonable and unfair to them personally.

"Based upon the above facts about the imperialist United States aggressor, the re-education and indoctrination program for American prisoners proceeds as planned" (*The Baylor Line* Vol. XIX, July–Aug., 1957).

Now let us go back to Major Mayer's report, based on his careful interrogation of these men. He indicated that the first step in the so-called "brain washing" was to do exactly the opposite of what American soldiers were expecting. The Chinese provided a warm, friendly welcome and brushed

aside, once and for all, any prospect of persecution and tor-
ture. The welcomer, a slender good-looking Chinese soldier
speaking perfect "American," said something like this:

> "We welcome you to the ranks of the people. We are
> happy and privileged to have liberated you from the im-
> perialist Wall Street warmongers who started this war.
> We have nothing against you personally. We know you
> don't want to be here any more than we do. We are not
> going to abuse you. We are going instead to offer you a
> proposition, a deal, a fair shake. The deal is this: you
> cooperate with us physically, don't get any ideas about
> our being your enemy, after all we're really people like
> you. Listen to us. Let us present to you our side of the
> world picture today of what we think is really going
> on here in Korea and back in your homes and with the
> great masses of people you've never had a chance to
> learn about. That's what we ask of you. In return for this
> there'll be no road crews, no coal mines. We'll just
> simply give you a chance to learn the truth as we know
> the truth to be. We're not even going to insist that you
> accept it. We ask only that you hear us out, which is
> only American fair play, and make up your own minds
> about what is true, and then as soon as the warmongers
> allow this senseless slaughter of innocent civilians to be
> ended, then we want you to go home to your own good
> homes and fine families and tell them the truth as you
> understand the truth to be" (*The Baylor Line*).

Instantly our men were off balance psychologically. Apparently some of them never regained their equilibrium.
Then the second phase began: segregation. Not only on a

color basis, but also from the point of view of aggressive leadership and unusual influence. All such poisonous influential individuals were removed to a "reactionary camp" and never allowed to return to their fellow soldiers. Major Mayer says, "Our first and most disturbing finding in general about the prisoners of war was the fact that it was necessary to segregate only one out of twenty American fighting men (this includes officers, non-commissioned officers and enlisted men) in order to deprive the other ninety-five per cent of any form of effective leadership. Only one out of every twenty Americans in this group, which I would like to emphasize was not the bottom of the manpower barrel, only one in twenty apparently thought it worthwhile to act on the basis of organization, of taking command, or of responding to command. They [the Communists] then had a group of approximately ninety-five per cent of the American soldiers leaderless. And with these [leaderless] people they [the Communists] set about then with their applied group psychology, not very mysterious psychology at that, designed basically to do one thing and one thing only" (*The Baylor Line*). And that one thing was to corrupt and interrupt communications between these men. They knew, as they know now, that once the system of communication between human beings, individually or collectively, is broken down, then that separated one, be it a nation or be it a lonely man, is at the mercy of the Communist plotter. Thus, the "self-criticism" technique, so highly developed and so thoroughly promoted in Communist areas, is set to work. The chief reason for the use of this vicious tool is the development of the "informer." In "self-criticism" one reaches the point where, out of a sense of duty to the State, one will inform on parent or friend, if such informing will help one become a better citizen of the State. To fail to inform may indicate that one has not thoroughly and honestly criticized oneself to the point where he will reveal information about an "enemy" of the State, whether relative or friend. Then, using their other standard tool, "rewarding the informer," the Communists manage to a greater or lesser degree to pit neighbor against neighbor or son against father. Hitler, too, used this method effectively, but the Communists have perfected it.

So, the American soldiers, leaderless to a large degree, were first allowed to spend endless hours and days alone and uninterrupted. During this time, as the Communists expected, the men shared secrets heretofore revealed to no man, much less to a stranger. When this process had reached a satisfactory stage, the next phase began. By taking these men aside for what they called "walking conferences," they managed to "brain-pick" from them, quite innocently enough, information about their fellow soldiers. Particularly were they interested in information that dealt with intimate and personal matters. When sufficient material had been gathered on as many men as possible, the Communists proceeded with the second step. They took the truth, revealed to them, and wove into it just enough lies to make an embarrassing, yet believable story. Then, in due time, the half-false, half-true story was circulated among the men. Almost immediately came the desired reaction: suspicion, distrust and hatred of one another. Every American soldier became confused as to who was and who was not a traitor, an informer and a collaborator. The saddest part of this process was that some of the informers actually felt that what they had done was their "civic duty" and that camp life would be a little easier as the result of giving away "innocent" non-military information about their fellow prisoners.

Immediately a curtain of silence fell over the camp. Voluntary solitary isolation became the residing place of these men, and their own fellow countryman became a dangerous potential enemy. Now the Communists had succeeded in this phase also. They had separated these men from the primary source of emotional support, their fellow Americans. And, by having cut off all incoming mail which might have boosted morale and by delivering all mail that would create the deeper wound of feeling forgotten or mistreated by supposedly loved ones at home, the vacuum in which each man lived became almost complete.

Now since nature hates a vacuum, the Communists prepared to move in. They moved into the lives and minds of these lonely, miserably betrayed men with a condensed educational program on the ills of Capitalism and the benefits of Communism. Lacking emotional support normally provided from without, these men became easy victims. With the average educational level of the ninth grade, the men were hardly immune to Communist propaganda.

What were the results? There were many. Let me list some of the *minor* results.

1. Though each American fighting man takes an oath to the effect that should he be captured by the enemy, he will escape or attempt to escape until either he succeeds or is killed or hostilities cease, yet these men became so docile that only one enemy soldier was needed to guard each one hundred Americans.

2. Fewer than a dozen documented attempts to escape occurred among these men.

3. Not one American soldier escaped from these camps.

4. Though medical care, food and clothing were provided to a degree not found in any P.O.W. camps during the Japanese conflict of World War II, yet these men died in greater numbers, percentagewise, than in any other prison camp or in any other prison in any war at any time in our history since the American Revolution. Thirty-eight per cent of them died. Why?

There were other "minor" results. But in the meantime, something else happened, which at first glance appeared to be an isolated event. Instead, it was to provide the Communists with proof that their "experiment" in Korea had actually succeeded. This event took place in New York when a Sergeant Gallagher from this same group was being tried for murder.

The charge was that he had ordered two men in his hut to be thrown out one bitterly cold Korean night because they were ill and the odor from their bodies nauseated him. One hour after their eviction from the hut they were frozen to death.

In the course of the trial, witnesses from the camp were brought in and asked for testimony. When the prosecuting attorney faced them, he asked questions somewhat like these:

"Did you know these men were sick?"

"Yes, sir."

"Did you know the defendant ordered them thrown out?"

"Yes, sir, I did."

"Did you know it was far below freezing outside?"

"Yes, sir."

And then the attorney asked this question, with something of the indignation he must have felt:

"Then, sir, if you knew these things why didn't you do something about it?"

The witness's answer caused the Communist to kiss their fingers with joy, they had succeeded! It could be done! For here is what witness after witness said:

"Well, frankly, sir, I didn't think it was any of my business."

None of his business! You can readily see why the Communists were elated. You can take an American and cut him off from his fellow Americans by spreading lies and half-truths between them. You can break down the traditional trust which an American feels for his own countryman. You can carelessly pin the words "pink" or "fellow traveler" or "pro-Communist" on a man. You can misquote, falsely quote, or deliberately twist what a man says until he has no confidence in himself or his fellow man. And his fellow man can be led to wonder if this man is to be forever permitted to walk the streets spreading Communist propaganda, and if no one else is going to do anything about it, he will. And he writes his unfounded suspicions to the F.B.I. Little by little we retreat from one another in one way or another.

Little by little we adopt the philosophy "it's every man for himself and the devil take the hindmost." Then the poison spreads to international affairs. The irresponsible public speaker who intimates, "France is a nation of drunkards; England is a fifth-rate power at best, on her way out; Italy is a nation of Communists; you can't trust the Germans or the Japanese, etc., etc.," on into the night. "We are the most hated nation in the world," he rattles on, after a two- or three-week trip to the Continent. "America has no friends in all the world. Our giveaway program has done us no good anywhere and in the meantime our nation is almost brought to bankruptcy by a loan-happy Congress and a giveaway President." Of course, this is not true. Not true at all. But by thus saying, and thus believing, we have moved closer and closer to the Communist trap. "Believe no man, trust no man. You have no friends, no emotional support. America is done for—going to the dogs—payola—rigged television programs—dishonest Congressmen, deceitful governmental officials, rotten Supreme Court; they are bombing churches and synagogues, swastikas are painted on the walls of public buildings, they call out hate the Jews, stop the foreign aid program, no Catholic for President, kill the Negroes; juvenile hoodlums, not safe on the streets of America, world's worst crime wave, tax evasion, world's highest divorce rate, breakdown of the American home, every man has his price." On and on the satanic diatribe goes, undermining and attempting to destroy our land and our world as we know it.

"And if you knew all these things," the Divine prosecutor asks, "why didn't you do something?" Are we to answer, "Well, frankly, sir, I didn't think it was any of my business"? God forbid! There is much we can do and much must be done, if we are to meet and overcome the clever enemy at our very gates today. If any man-made plan has not been tried in the past, history does not reveal it. Every alliance and every type of treaty and agreement imaginable has been tried over and over and over again. And every one of them has ultimately failed. The one thing that has not been tried, at least in the last thousand years, has been an all-out advance on the non-Christian world by the people of God. And never have so many waited for so long and received so little.

That is why the man who calls the missionary "the meddler" strikes a small blow at the one possible and untried way by which we may change the world; by changing men's hearts, we may change the world. And that's why the man who says he doesn't believe the Christian people are really serious or have ever made a serious effort to reach the world is, by his very pessimism, taking away just that much emotional and moral support which the Christian needs to become dead in earnest about his part in world Christian missions.

And that's part of the story why Christian concern and the Christian sense of responsibility still stand as Communism's number one road block. They know Christian concern must never be allowed to become aroused to the point of really doing something about "preaching Christ to the nations." The half-hearted effort in which we Christians have so long engaged cannot long stand against a subtle, wise and evil disease like Communism. We must either activate our forces, or abdicate our stand. We are not going to be able to fool the world much longer.

Up to this point what have we done? Let us review and summarize our efforts.

We have spent billions trying to buy the world's friendship and to dry up Communism's breeding pools. But all we seem to have succeeded in doing is to provide ourselves with a momentary stopgap; this will stand only as long as the taxpayers of the free world can bear the load. In the meantime, the malignancy goes deeper and deeper into a generation, almost two generations, in more than half of the world's population who have never known anything but the Communist way of life. Each day that half of the world remains ignorant of a better way of life, the threat to our world grows greater.

Suppose those billions of dollars, or some major portion of them, had been spent to export the one commodity which we possess, which Russia does not possess, namely, our Christian concern and the Christian Gospel? Though the Russians can match us bag of wheat for bag of wheat, and hydroelectric dam for hydroelectric dam, they cannot match Bible for Bible or Christian missionary for Christian missionary. Suppose we were to mount the massive offensive heretofore described on a world wide scale to carry the message of the angels to the shepherds that first Christmas, "For unto you is born this day in the city of David, a Saviour who is Christ the Lord"? Just suppose!

But the strange thing is that in this present moment of desperate crisis, while our President girdles the globe on a marvelous mission of peace and while our Secretary of State whirls from country to country making new treaties or alliances, or patching up old ones; and while the reporters of world events stand at the listening posts of the world with bated breath hoping to be the first to hear the opening shot in not only the world's third World War, but its last as well, our one greatest weapon lies kicked into the corner by the world's statesmen as useless and powerless. The One Weapon is the one the Soviet Government hopes we will not use, for there is no known defense against it in the knowledge of mankind.

We are suffering from national paralytic blindness brought

on by intense fear. That it should affect our national and international political figures is bad enough. But for it to have affected our spiritual leaders is far, far worse. So deeply have some of them been affected that there is, on their part, either the unwillingness or the inability to discuss the possibility of a coordinated strategy of worldwide advance on a solid front against Christianity's most dangerous enemy—Atheistic Communism. Why?

Well, one reason, often and quite honestly given, is the resultant danger such a militant move would have upon those Christians who are now behind the "iron" or "bamboo" curtains of the world.

There is a fear (real or imagined, who knows?) that should we become too aggressive in our efforts to win men to Christ behind these curtains, those won, whether recently or not, would become the object of persecution and death. With this threat of retaliation hanging over our Christian brothers' heads, atrocity after atrocity is committed, and sneer after sneer is thrown, and no one dares to rise and challenge for fear of "retaliation." But those who study the past and particularly that part of the past recorded in the Bible will find that no threat of this nature meant a snap of the finger to Paul or John or any of the Christian martyrs of the early church. Paul preached and John wrote against a background very similar to the background of today. A totalitarian government of worldwide proportions threatened horrible death to any believer in "the way," but instead it was against the background of the screams of the dying and the flames of persecution that the finest chapters of Christian history were written.

Therefore, it seems to me, someone should question the

wisdom of the present philosophy of "don't antagonize the enemy and thus make it more difficult for our Christian brothers within his grasp." Someone should remember that the blood of the martyrs still may be the seed-bed for the ultimate victory over Communism. To think so, it may be claimed, is easy for us on this side of the curtain. But to assume the privilege of such an assumption and deprive our brother of his rightful heritage is not only to be presumptuous, but it is also to play directly into the hands of the enemy.

Such is the case for the timid. And such has been the case for so long that many thoughtful people seem to be convinced that foreign Christian missions and Western influence as a whole are fighting a rearguard action in an overall worldwide defeat. They feel that we are being led by a sizable group in government and church circles who, if we are not careful, will negotiate this nation out of existence. And they will do so to avoid "war" and assure "survival." "War" we already have, vicious and powerful, and survival in this war will not depend on the "negotiated peace" or the "counsels of fear." Survival will be assured *only* when Christian people of all persuasions convince their hesitant, timid or traitorous leaders that they want to "advance and attack" with the Christian Gospel regardless of those who would suffer behind or in front of the world's drawn curtains. If a real and gigantic offense cannot be mounted by the Christian people of our world in the near future, then the future of our world looks dark indeed. For free people can enjoy their freedom off in a corner, only just so long, playing, working or discussing, and before they know it, their freedom is gone. And in the meantime, those behind the Iron Curtain whose lives they sought to protect by remaining quiet, are still there. The only difference will be—we shall be there too!

The critics' first charge against the foregoing statements will be "oversimplification." "Oversimplification" because all the facts are not known nor are they all taken into consideration. Let the critics then consider the following statement:

It is a fact that the one thing we possess exclusively is the success story of a Christian culture, its ups and downs, flaws and faults notwithstanding. And concurrently, we possess a faith, sometimes vital, sometimes not so vital, in a living God. Therefore, though Communism may be able successfully to compete in agriculture or heavy industry, it cannot compete with the explosive power which we can export, on a massive scale, of the Christian message of forgiveness and redemption.

SIX

Christian Concern and Present-day Foreign Missions

THE RISE OR FALL OF CHRISTIAN CONCERN CARRIES WITH IT the destiny of our world as we know it. Somehow this fact has escaped the notice of millions.

In a way, it would be amusing, if it were not pitiable, when we hear grown men and women lamenting the "lack of purpose" in American life. ("Purpose" is only another term commonly used in the place of "Christian concern.") The lament is true, and there is nothing amusing about it. Recently, Sylvan Myer, editor of the *Gainesville* (Ga.) *Times,* wrote, "They've told us we have to sacrifice luxuries to carry out our job to the world. We're willing. But nobody tells us what to sacrifice and nobody tells us the purpose." At the same time, Homer McEwen, pastor of the First Congregational Church in Atlanta, says, "We have lost our national thrust toward a moral society."

Watching the unfolding of what Adlai Stevenson called "the National Drift," one cannot help but wonder why our leaders do not recognize the symptoms and go back to the founding fathers for the cure. When the Declaration of Independence was written, the very words were afire with purpose. When the Pilgrims set sail from the Continent, it was as if the sails of the tiny ships were filled with the winds of purpose. And when the pioneers headed west over our vast new land, they endured hardships that would kill the modern generation. They moved with purpose, the same purpose that drove Abraham, Moses, David, Jesus, Paul and countless thousands who indelibly wrote their names on the hallmark of history. "We are sent by Almighty God."

With this driving force like a cold and cutting wind, that caused men to set out to do the impossible, knowing they were somehow linked irrevocably with the God of history, they crossed seas, climbed mountains and suffered incredibly for their cause. The cause—the cause! This was the sum total of existence. Today, men have lost the sense of cause and have thus lost a sense of responsibility to themselves, their fellow men and to that mother of destiny, history herself.

No man could do modern civilization a greater service than to provide a worthy cause for the expending of human energies and life. Yet, strangely and pitifully, we live in an ocean of cause—the bringing of our world to a thorough knowledge of the God of all history. To re-align ourselves with the tides of human destiny is like a great missile taking a bead on the distant star. If modern man could rediscover the values of Luther and David Livingstone and William Carey! If the spirit of Albert Schweitzer and others of this modern generation of could-be giants could once again see clearly a divine destiny in life—the searching for a cause would be at an end. There is still available the power and energy that were released and continued in chain-reaction through those first centuries after Christ. Look back on it now without sentimentality: the going forth of the twelve disciples stands as one of the finest moments in the history of the human race. "Go ye therefore into all the world," He said and they took Him literally! No danger, no hardship was too much. They crossed every known sea, climbed every necessary mountain, they faced death as one faces a new day. As a consequence, they managed to turn history around and rewrite the philosophy of Rome, Greece and Alexandria.

A cause—an idea—a faith—that set them on the track. And there was no turning them back. The world's greatest idea had a firm grip on their imagination. "We can change a man's way of life and his eternal destination. We can change the course of governments, overthrow despots and rewrite history. There are no obstacles that can stop us, no iron curtain that can halt our progress, no threats to us or our comrades that will change our plans." No matter what the cynical may say, the world has never seen anything like it, and nothing of a different nature will ever equal it. And the hope of our world, the repossession of purpose, lies squarely in the area of the reassumption of the ideals of those desperate men, the Apostles, who could not but do the will of God as they saw it, come what may.

Certainly there has been a lag. A very long lag—far too long. But the lag has not and cannot be traced to a dying out of the applicability of the Christian Gospel to the century in which we live. It is not that church people don't want to do the job of world missions; it is that they've been misled. The meanings of the words "challenge" and "vision" and "lost world" have become identified with human frailty instead of Divine Command. If we cannot preach to the world, in a powerful, persuasive and world-reaching manner, then why were we commanded to do so by our Lord? Have our leaders come to the place where they have actually been able to square their limitations with the Divine possibilities inherent in a genuine, real honest-to-God worldwide mission program? And if they have, haven't they taken a lot on themselves to commit the rest of us to such a flabby, unimaginative, half-hearted effort? When our leaders speak, they often mention a paradox that is inconsistent with world need. Here is how the situation is often stated: "We have more mission volunteers, highly qualified volunteers, acceptable and trained volunteers, than we have money to send them." Here God is busy calling up and preparing leadership and there are more, by the hundreds, perhaps by the thousands, available, and something has prevented the necessary funds from being supplied. I think I know enough about the Christian heart to know that when it is challenged, when it is set afire by someone who has the Pauline vision of a world that lies in sin, when the heart can give its material resources to the actual direct winning of that dying world, then nothing, absolutely nothing, can prevent it from giving. Some men, who have had that vision, have caused the poor to take rings from their fingers and drop them in the collection plate. Unbelievable sacrifices can and have and will be made, when our nation comes to see a vision and a plan to carry out that vision. A plan in which they can have complete confidence. A plan that is scripturally sound and carried out by spiritually qualified laymen and ministers.

First, we must see the need and the plan, and then we must tell it so others can see it. This is the method. And when it is followed, by qualified and dedicated people, the God of this universe will match men and money and arrest the dreadful drift of the frightened millions who have lost their purpose. Let the worldly-wise sophisticate be ignored. And forget the so-called wise man who looks down his nose at the spiritual quickening which he has never had, which caused and continues to cause men to right wrong, seek to live pure and honestly before God and man, and sincerely try to set the spiritual world of mankind back on its safe and well-known foundation—a firm and living belief in a personal God.

Here let us make some general observations. Some say that the present situation in world missions is comparable to the situation presently existing between the United States and Russia. While Russia is doing everything in her power to destroy us and all we stand for, we are so committed to our *present* way of life we cannot find the new attitudes and methods we need to defend ourselves. True, we have produced, through trial and error, a mode of living and working which, for the present, meets our needs rather well. But we cannot stop the law of change. We have found no method by which we can halt history in its headlong flight. "Give me liberty or give me death" paints a picture that admirably suited our forefathers' needs and correctly stated the attitude of a minority at least. But we have come to a new period in man's existence when there is a distinct possibility that one can lose his liberty and not die. It is not an either-or proposition any longer. There is a third possibility, and that is that one may awaken one morning to find oneself in a conquered world and having to live in it, like it or not. Patrick Henry spoke of a battle to the death with an armed enemy that could or would be shot with a gun or a cannon. We face an enemy that hides behind our own Bill of Rights and often seeks election to our political offices and makes attempt after attempt to rewrite our laws in order to provide him with more "freedom" through which he may ultimately produce our downfall and his victory.

Consequently, the methods of protecting our freedoms have broadened. Those who are called upon to fight now number every one of us who believes in God and the dignity and worth of the immortal soul of man. The fight against the enemy is every freeman's fight and every freeman should be expected to do his part. But the world mission program of our Christian denominations has not come around to embracing the all-out means of protecting our land, our faith and our children we advocate.

In a way, the present program is as simple as was Patrick Henry's famous saying. One or two or even a handful of missionaries move quietly into a land and there they call about them a few children and teach them the story of Jesus. Well and good. But this cannot be the method with which we shall fight and overthrow satanic communism and the powerful foe of materialism. World mission effort must be geared to world affairs. Especially it must be geared to American policy on foreign affairs. If this is not necessary, why are we told that the segregation problem and the status of the Negro in America are directly affecting our mission work abroad? Can we honestly expect the world to overlook a difference between what we believe and practice in our own land and what we preach abroad? Of course, most men grant that Americans live in a "fish bowl of world opinion." They will admit that what the missionary faces on foreign soil is in some measure colored by impressions gained from published pronouncements of some of America's so-called leading

"Christians" and political figures. Then why do these same people frown on the idea that "world missions must be geared to world affairs and American foreign policy"?

By this we do not mean that the doctrines of our faith are to be compromised until they become mere tools of unscrupulous politicians. To the contrary, we are speaking of a world mission policy so realistic and widely held, that what the Christian people of our Western World hold as true will be dynamic in the shaping of our nation's planning and executing in the arena of international affairs. So far, our preciously held doctrine of separation of church and state has prevented this interlocking of motives and this osmosis of thought from taking place on a wide and effective scale.

In the meantime the situation deteriorates by our own confession. Mass communication has never been employed on an effective worldwide scale by Christian forces. Only a tiny fraction of the Voice of America broadcasts are used to tell the story of the Christian meaning of life, though hours are devoted to the praises of capitalism. Yet we know and avow that the underlying basis of our system of Government is Hebraic-Christian religion. The manager of one of the world's most powerful radio stations, located in a pro-communist nation, managed to show something of his frustration when he said, "Even the religious broadcasts from America weaken your case over here." He named America's most widely known evangelist who uses the radio considerably as an evangelistic instrument here and abroad. He said, "Sunday after Sunday he points out all the weaknesses and shortcomings of America. He tells of moral deterioration and sin in high places. He speaks of national immorality and lack of cause on the part of America. When he says those things in

America, he may hope to spur you Americans to seek to return to God and that is well and good. But when it is broadcast overseas it lessens the small hope and confidence some of us have that America is our last hope." The editor of a newspaper in Japan said, "If what I read in some of your news magazines is true, then Russia tells the truth when she tells the Eastern bloc that America is rotten to the core." Again, the quotations from businessmen and government officials here in our own country are carefully sifted by Radio Moscow and the Communist press of the world; then they are given the slightest twist and rebroadcast and reprinted in the newspapers.

That little twist is enough to do great damage. For instance, when the writer was in South Africa a short time ago, a case in point arose. Our government had insisted, and rightly so, that the Salk polio vaccine should be made available to any country willing to fulfill certain conditions: i.e., governmental control, no commercial sale (do everything possible to keep it off the black market). This idea was perfectly correct. And we honor our country for insisting on it. However, a news article in the South African press had as its headline, "U. S. Government Refuses Polio Vaccine To South Africa," and the article read, "Strings and conditions tied to the availability of U. S. Salk Polio Vaccine continue to prevent the South African people from having the benefit of Dr. Salk's famous discovery. In the meantime, ten new cases of polio were announced in Port Elizabeth alone this week." The damage was inestimable. This same anti-U. S. material was printed all over the world. And our missionaries faced this new obstacle in their day's work. In the light of this type of misrepresentation, why have religious groups not taken advantage of international radio facilities and possibilities? Isn't that one way we could spread the message of Christ and give a more accurate picture of what the Christian people of our nation and culture stand for?

Another observation pertains to this area. Americans have had to assume the role of the world's image reflection. We are supposed to be the epitome of freedom and to exhibit proper race relations, substantial industrial leadership, an all-wise government policy, etc., etc. And our shortcomings are what causes the world to become so furious with us at times. It's not a hatred for America as such. It is anger that we shatter the mirror of hope into which the world looks so yearningly. We have the biggest cars, the biggest corporations, the most money—and then, in their eyes, we act so small. Some may say that as shattering as this may be, the sooner we destroy the "Santa Claus" idea of Uncle Sam around the world, the sooner the world's population will begin to grow up, and the better off we all shall be in the long run. This may be so. But in the meantime the ideal of Christian leadership in the world will have taken an awful beating. The truth is, we don't live in such a "foreign world" as some may think, including the Communists. Stand in the streets of Japan, Korea, Singapore, Ceylon and India as well as in other parts of the world and one impression will grow increasingly vivid. The masses of the people in our world have no real interest in politics as such. They fight a twenty-four-hour-a-day battle for no more than the actual necessities of life.

> Home in a hole
> Rice in the bowl,
> It's tomorrow too soon.

This is the unspoken cry of these masses. They are no more Communists than we are. They could not care less. But they will follow anyone who will give them something to help them live a little better. For instance, Nehru, the Indian leader, is not playing East against West in some vicious underhanded way. Nehru is simply getting help wherever he can get help and thus he furnishes the world a perfect picture of the mind and politics of the man in the street of Madras or Bombay.

Actually, I have never seen better capitalists than in the East. Every one of them is a potential self-employed businessman. The East abounds in street corner, curbstone, backside, top-of-the-head, palm-of-the-hand merchants buying some noodles here, selling them there, exchanging pocket combs, fountain pens, shoestrings, hair oil, sweets, fruits, meat or fried intestines. Anything they can find they sell, make a little profit and then divide the profit two ways—live on a portion of it and plow the rest back into the business. The rich Chinese merchant who boomed "Tiger Balm" in a multi-million dollar business is more the ideal of the man of the East than any government leader or religious leader that part of the world has ever seen or will ever see. Russia can give and give and give but she cannot change human nature. A man is a born capitalist. He wants to buy cheap and sell at a profit, and if possible, as soon as possible, he wants to branch out into another field. To think that he can be taught, trained or forced to feel or be otherwise is as profitable as trying to dam up Niagara Falls with spit balls.

That is why men like Albert Schweitzer have thrown themselves into the breach. They have only one candle to light and they light it. To sit back and wait for men everywhere to become as disgusted as the Hungarians is too cruel to contemplate.

There are at least two methods used to conquer a land or a people: all-out assault or fifth-column infiltration. Our government in World War II used the assault in the Pacific to great advantage. A target was picked. Chiefs of Army, Navy, Air Corps and Marines met, planned, selected their various roles, agreed on a timetable, chose spots of invasion and even planned so far as to have a military government selected, trained and ready to go in with the assault. The Air Force reconnoitered and supplied aerial photographs. The Navy studied charts and found harbors and beaches. The Army and Marines planned the waves of landing, etc.

It seems to me that to attempt to take a country, or even a specific area like Singapore or Sumatra for Christ, a meeting of the Chiefs of Staff of all those who might be able to play a part in the assault should be called. A "grand strategy" should be worked out, a timetable set, a list drawn up of essential needs and supplies, spots selected for first attack and second attack, etc. Who will make up the first wave of the assault?

Perhaps a team of laymen and ministers could first survey the field, government regulations, and government recognition. Is there an influential Christian man, a businessman, who could go in and smooth the way? Is there some Christian in the U. S. Embassy there whose friendship we can expect? What are previous unpleasant experiences suffered by the population in the name of religion? Extensive survey committees could work out all these and hundreds of other details while trained experts in religions of the world could make a quiet and careful and thorough study on-the-spot of the problems of that country's particular brand of Buddhism or Hinduism. Then when these surveys of people, government, language, religion, laws and possible friends have been made, then our foreign mission boards would begin an all-out drive for missionaries (for whatever number it had previously been decided should go) for that particular country. It may be that the initial wave should be ten people. So the Seminary senior classes are screened first. Perhaps one year later, ten more should go in. Seminaries' junior classes are approached. It will have been determined ahead of time just how many specialists will be necessary for this particular area: doctors, nurses, evangelists, teachers, and also how many contract workers (we might call them C.W.'s) could be used, and of what classification—builders, linguists, musicians, etc. Medical schools, junior colleges and senior colleges would be notified and word would be sent everywhere. In the meantime, prayer programs could be arranged through Brotherhoods and W.M.U.'s. Churches would not be praying "for our foreign missionaries around the world," they would be praying month in and month out for one particular field. Out of this home base activity and amidst our churches, God would call the necessary leadership and prepare them to meet the demands of the hour.

That's the kind of program Christ had in mind when He spoke of the militant church that was to be His—the church before whose onslaught the gates of Hell would fall.

Otherwise, it is our opinion, and we think we could make it "stand up in court," that we are wasting man- and woman-power in far too many places and cases by sending them out two by two instead of seventy by seventy. We talked to older missionaries on two fields we visited, missionaries soon to retire, who said, "It's been a case of 'too little too late.' We can't help but wonder whether we have accomplished as much as we were capable of accomplishing if we had had an adequate program, a sufficient staff and proper planning." When we asked if there had been a "grand strategy" worked out before they came or after they arrived, they laughed. Then they recovered themselves to say, "We just left that in the Lord's hands and sought His guidance in daily prayer." But to the question, "Have you felt that if you had to do it over again you would make certain definite changes in our program of procedure," they answered "yes" without qualification. "There is a better way of doing this," said one young male missionary of four years' service, "I am using up the best years of my life and the results are so small. If we only had adequate staff and if we only had a general plan in mind that would appear to have some chance of success. As it is, one man is trying to do the work of twenty and in addition to this tremendous burden, I must try to plan for ten, fifteen or twenty years ahead. I can't do it." Then he said, "I'm just putting one foot in front of the other and trusting God for the rest." Such activity does not show that we are being "as wise as serpents and harmless as doves" in our "advance" on a world that is growing more pagan every hour of the day.

An all-out assault would employ every means of communication, every tool of finance, industry and invention, every trained mind the evangelical Christians of America could muster. We would need:

Books prepared ahead of time in native tongues on various subjects, to be given to the people. English-native dictionaries provided, to help those who might come only because they want to learn English.

Music books and simple courses in piano playing prepared to reach those who might come only because of their love of music.

Medical diagnosis of the simple medical problems of that area, in language the native could understand and with information as to how they might find treatment through the Christian Medical Clinics for these and more serious medical problems.

Simple manuals containing problems of farmers, dairymen, etc., in that particular area, and answers to them.

Almost any serviceman who saw foreign service can testify that many of these materials were prepared ahead of time by the Army and given to the men prior to invasion of a particular area.

That brings us to the most important part of this all-out assault program: advance training and briefing.

A code name could be given to a particular area rather than using the country's name. Then, when the grand strategy, over-all planning, dates, materials, etc., had been prepared, the entire body of personnel (those ready now, soon to be ready, or those who had volunteered but still had no more than two years of college to go) would be called together for a month of briefing and study. At least a month would be devoted to absorbing native habits, food, customs, medical problems, etc., and a part of that period devoted to discussing, revising and agreeing on the "grand strategy" which has been prepared beforehand. Subsequent meetings for further training would be set up, involving the return of one of those who had gone out to the field who would further brief those who have volunteered but are still training. Each country would be treated as a unit, each unit trying to recruit others to fit into the spots still open in the table of organization; the churches would be kept informed of progress, needs and problems, while a constant stream of prayer would go up to God from all over our land for the mission.

SEVEN

Foreign Policy for Foreign Missions

IN AN ADDRESS DELIVERED BEFORE THE FIFTH ANNUAL All-Jesuit Alumni Dinner in Washington, D.C., in 1953, John Foster Dulles, Secretary of State, said, "In my experience, those who are most positive about political problems are able to be positive only because they do not know all the relevant facts. Those who are most harsh in their judgments are able to be harsh for that same reason. When the whole of a problem is known, solutions become excessively difficult and judgments are not easily made." In the light of this and other statements, apparently profound, one would gather that in order to comment on serious problems of a political or international nature, one must know all the facts involved. Since, for instance, in Mr. Dulles' case, he alone, with the possible exception of the President, had all the facts, any comment or judgment by any one else on these events would be faulty, per se.

Such, of course, is simply not so. In fact, the very opposite may be true. If one were to study history only a little, one would be surprised to learn that "trees may get in the way so much, that the forest cannot be seen." Secretary Dulles may often have been blinded to solutions because of the innumerable facts which he possessed. Someone has observed that one may succeed in reaching remarkable solutions to problems because one didn't know that it "couldn't be done."

So it would seem in the area of world missions. Were one to listen to the experts, one would conclude that there are so many ramifications to the problem to which this book addresses itself, that a layman cannot hope to speak on the matter and make any sense. This simply is not so. The outstanding fact, reduced to its essence, is that the world is in the most dangerous predicament within the knowledge of man. Though for many centuries men have tried every means known to them to stop war and live in peace together, they have only succeeded in waging bigger and bigger wars with more and more destruction. Alliances, leagues of nations, balances of power, disarmament programs, armament programs, world courts, etc., ad nauseam notwithstanding. Periodically, the world *takes* a blood-bath. This moral and spiritual madness that sets in periodically has finally brought us to the point where we have entered a sequence of events from which there appears to be no return.

Of course, there are those who argue that this time it will be different. This time, "We have the United Nations and the United States is a member, and with the wisdom gained from the past and the knowledge that there can be no 'winner' this time, war is at last doomed to the limbo of the forgotten and detested past." Thus spoke one of our leading scientists recently. Since his voice has been added to the chorus of other scientists, who have similarly warned us in the past, one can hardly overlook such a weighty statement. However, there are mitigating circumstances involved here.

One, at least, tends to cancel out the meaningfulness and sincerity of the scholarly broadsides delivered by the scientific community. This mitigating fact is a factor in our favor. It is that for the first time in history the scientist has created a weapon that, when used, will kill him also. Heretofore, he worked in the safety of a laboratory from which issued a stream of destruction to be loosed on the world's population. But his own safety was never at stake. As a matter of fact, with each increase in fire-power that he devised, with each added ability to destroy enemies, the scientist rose in value and estimation in the eyes of the community, so that today, almost every nation capable of doing so is expediting the production of scientific brains, at the maximum quantity and speed. And, for the first time in the history of science, its leaders are trying to put on "the brakes" in the frenzy of weapons-production. The only obvious reason is that the formerly safe laboratory and research center is no longer a haven for quiet study and further development. The truth is, the scientists are scared. The frankenstein they have produced has now turned upon them and they have come streaming out of the laboratories, shouting "help, murder, police." Looking on from the outside, one could not help being amused, if the situation were not so grim. Now the observation just given is corroborated partially by the status of the men shouting "help" and by the leaning of modern science more and more toward a more-than-nodding acquaintance with heartfelt religious faith. This, of course, is another tremendous factor in our favor.

Actually, it is doubtful whether within the knowledge of man, there has been a time when men of science have openly avowed a faith in God in such numbers as at the present.

They, too, are looking, not at the difficulties involved, as Mr. Dulles would have urged, but at the stark reality—we cannot find world peace in atomic war. But, since the atom-smashing devices are here, and a general ability to create atom bombs is in possession of several nations, we cannot abolish them and the knowledge of how to produce them. Since this knowledge represents the ultimate in power, duplicating the power of the sun itself, another and completely different avenue of solution must be found, or we are lost. What the scientists, who have thus spoken out, are doing is to lend their tremendous prestige to leading the world to the only other avenue open to us that promises solution, the only other avenue, at least, that has not been really tried.

While the Roman Catholic Church prepares to call a council to restudy and consolidate its efforts, the Protestant Churches of America and the world should be preparing a study-council of equal distinction and scope to meet the demands of this new and fearful day in which we live. Not to do so is tacit agreement that we cannot work together, or that we do not care to. Either could be fatal.

It is my sincere hope that a group of men in the scientific, political, business, literary and religious communities could be banded together officially or unofficially, outside any such organization as the World Council of Churches or the National Council of Churches, to pool their knowledge, concern and resources in providing a "laboratory" for work, a "forum" for study and a clearinghouse for information to all religious groups seeking assistance. This council on world missions would have its members selected by the various denominations now active in any appreciable degree in world missions and would be composed of men and women from both the laity and the ministry but with never more than two-thirds being drawn from either category. Acting in a similar capacity as the President's Committee on National Security, they would advise only; they would have no power other than that derived from the prestige of the members, individually and collectively, and the standing they gained by the wisdom and integrity of their work. With a rule limiting the period of service on the Council for each member, there would be an assurance of new imagination and skills as new members are added. If this or some similar group were thus organized, and if their power was limited to counsel only, then for the first time in the history of world missions, there would be a means by which worldwide coordination of effort could be achieved without the stigma of force or organic union being involved.

World opinion is waiting for such a move on the part of Christian Protestant America. And, once this Council has proven itself to be an honorable body of people who have risen above national and sectarian restrictions in order to "get on with the job," then slowly, to be sure, but surely, we might make, not a reversal of our course, but a slow swing back toward a just and durable peace based upon the principles found not only in the New Testament but also in the Torah, the Koran and Confucius. Good men of almost all Christian faiths seem to agree that:

1) No single denomination or faith has a corner of the truth, and
2) since we have reached a point in history where it is return or perish, and
3) because all other methods of success in living together on this planet have been tried and failed, and because

4) we believe that the winning of men to Christ actually produces not "nice men" but instead, "new men,"

5) then we must find a way to work together toward
that end.

And we must do so immediately. By "we" I mean the
Christian Community of our Western Civilization. If we don't
work together, we will have failed our day and generation.

Every Christian is agreed that the Commission of the
Church is to take the Gospel to the World. "You shall be my
witnesses in Jerusalem and in all Judea and Samaria and to
the end of the earth" (Acts 1:8, RVS). The Communist
Party also conceives of itself as being worldwide in its reach.
And the two ideologies are running head-on into each other
with an impact which will become more evident and more
violent all over the world as the Communist force grows.

It's a conservative statement to say that Christianity today
is not a major world force in political or economic affairs
anywhere in the world. There was a time, centuries ago,
when it was. But it isn't today. It has been relegated to the
past by the financial and economic and industrial world as
not much more than a museum piece. And Christianity does
not play an active and vital and forceful part in any of the
fields of global politics of our world today.

It may be that there are many reasons for this. One is that
it's possible that our present-day church program is not
geared to world need. It's possible that we've failed to relate
the people of our churches to a lost world. And from this
single fact alone, we may reap a terrible harvest. The present-
day church program is identical in many respects to the
program that's been used in one way or another, to one

extent or another, for many, many scores of decades. Over all, our present-day church program has had very little change. As a consequence, a minister stands in his pulpit and preaches to a church today that is usually organized into at least four divisions: a Sunday School, a training organization, a women's group and a brotherhood for the men. What part these divisions play in world missions depends first on the preacher himself and, secondly, on the man or woman who stands before a class, or a training union, or a study group in the women's work, or a group of the brotherhood. Whether the organizational life of our churches is related to a world mission program hangs on whether the pulpit itself has the world on its heart or not. It is left to you to answer whether it does in the large majority of cases. Granting that it does, it seems possible that in addition to these four organizations, all of which are rendering tremendous service in evangelism, Bible study and training, we could implement their work with another type of approach to the world mission problem.

It seems that someone might address himself to the re-evaluation of the present church program, in order that in addition to the present organizations, the entire congregation could be divided into "areas of study" groups. Thus, in the average congregation, there would be a chosen group designated to study and relate themselves and the local church to the world mission program of Africa, as carried on by the foreign mission boards. Another committee would be designated to study and report to the church on the work of Europe. Other committees would be designated to study and report to the church the mission work of the denomination in other areas of the world. They would also, from time to time, send members of the congregation to visit these mission fields and to bring back personal reports of what they saw and what was being done with the money, and what could be done by the local church to increase the effectiveness of the work abroad. But as of this writing, our people in our churches drop their offering in the collection plate, and perhaps nine out of ten give no thought to what it does or whose life it will touch or what Seminary student it might bless or what soul it might save. This is a catastrophe. It is the age-old error of people giving to church budgets rather than *through* them to world needs. Obviously, it is not the fault of the local church or the denominational budget as such; it is the fault of our mission education program on the local level.

When Paul felt his call to be a missionary to the Gentiles, he struck out, going from country to country. He crossed national boundaries and faced language barriers that were difficult, but he met the demands of his day—wherever there were people to whom he could preach, he went. And when the dispersion hit the church at Jerusalem and Christians were scattered in every direction, they scattered to preach. Today we have a handy and easy manner, for instance, of designating approximately 1300 people to serve our nine million Southern Baptists around the world and to preach the Gospel to two and a half billion people of this world. Far too handy, in fact, and we all know it can't be done. But we know a better job could be done if personnel and money were made available in sufficient quantities, and our program enlarged on a vast enough scale.

But what have world mission needs to do with the man in the pew in the average church? I'm afraid it has very little meaning to him. He gives it a thought once in a while, but nothing is seriously entertained in his mind about what he might do to change the picture. And it appears that with the threats we face in our world today, with all we've been told over and over again by men who ought to know, steps should be taken immediately to remedy this dangerous state of affairs. What tomorrow holds for us may be an unbelievably desperate experience. And what are the people who serve the Lord Jesus Christ doing to gird themselves to meet world needs? We appear to be doing very little.

For instance, it's doubtful whether our present-day methods of foreign mission work are geared to solve or even to attack the serious problems that face our world today. The Christian mission programs of America's major denominations have no joint, long-range strategy program. No committee of laymen and ministers concerned with national and international security have sat down to plan a program for the next twenty-five or fifty years. Very little attention apparently has been given to a study of population trends or to an attempt to try to find what's going to happen in relation to the Christian message, to the great masses of population in India and China and other areas of the earth; or to find the strategic cities where we might more thoroughly organize and staff our Christian effort and thus be better prepared to meet the threat of Communism wherever it may strike.

The author was a member of the staff of the Air Force Chief of Chaplains in the Pentagon during World War II, and sat in on the planning program of the ultimate attack on Okinawa as well as on other islands of the Pacific. We sat, we made no contribution, but we sat and listened. We lis-

tened to these men who made plans to call upon every
resource of our country. They determined to find all those
who spoke the languages of the intended areas of invasion.
They had to find the people who knew their history, their
customs, their diseases. Then they began to prepare and
train the officials they would need. They trained a city council, a police force, a water engineer, an electrical engineer.
In other words, they prepared themselves to meet the
medical and economic and social needs of the areas which
they planned to capture two or three years hence. And
as they planned their resources and marshaled their forces,
they called upon men of ability and talent from every area
where they were needed. They stockpiled their supplies and
their personnel carefully until they were thoroughly prepared. And then one day our battleships surrounded the
chosen targets and poured their shells on the shoreline. Later
on, planes came over and bombarded, and then landing craft
skidded upon the beach, and the island was ultimately captured. And as they were invaded there moved into the places
of responsibility the people who had been chosen and prepared to see that things went as they should, and that the
area would be controlled.

Now the same sort of massive attack in one way or another
should be designed and planned by Christian forces of our
Western Christian civilization. It should be planned by all
men who really believe in preaching evangelistically in the
name of the Lord Jesus Christ. And this planning should
provide some way whereby we could look ahead and locate
the strategic areas and cities of the world, and the peoples
of the world that can be most easily influenced. And then
would come the stockpiling of supplies and personnel. A

careful sifting of our high schools would help us locate the boys and girls who have dedicated their lives to the cause of Christian missions in their local churches. Go through our colleges and locate the men and women who feel themselves called of God into foreign missions. Go into seminaries and locate them in their very first year, if possible. Then, having found the personnel, we assume the task of matching, at the earliest feasible moment, the person to the job. When this is done, special language schools would be available for training these choice people in the languages they will have to use, years before they land on those shores.

A missionary on one mission field reported that when he landed there, he couldn't even say "hello" to the people with whom he was to serve for the rest of his life. And so our people should be trained far in advance. Let summer periods be set aside when young people could be sent to an encampment or assembly and there taught the background and history of various countries in which we now serve and those in which we hope to serve. With these and other methods already instituted by the various mission boards, we would be far better prepared to meet and overcome the snarling boast of the swaggering communist, who says, "Christianity has had its day."

But as the years have gone by, it seems that it has been either "slow down" or "get out" of country after country, so that our mission forces in many of the areas which we now occupy could not give you assurance that they will be serving there this time next year.

Now this is a serious matter. It affects the life of our children. It affects the life of every Christian in our world. Somewhere, someone is going to have to be willing to pick up the challenge and match the men and supplies necessary to face the challenge that threatens our very existence. When will it happen? We don't know. Nor does anyone else seem to know. But let us use one possible example that might help determine an answer. There are hundreds of dedicated Christian doctors who might be willing, if given the opportunity, to go overseas to areas designated by the various mission boards for three, six or even nine months, perhaps to act as a relief for present mission personnel needing furlough, or as supplementary forces, on a temporary basis. When these men came back from these mission fields to their local churches, they doubtless would be on fire for the Lord, and as a result of their witness, they would bring into our churches that New Testament zeal which they so desperately need, and which they once so wonderfully possessed. For every time churches have had a great world mission program on their heart, and a burning desire to win the world to Christ, they catch fire. And when the people of Christ are on fire, the world begins to get warm again.

There are qualified teachers who possibly would be glad to go, if they could go for one-, two- or three-year periods. It is possible we could gather together people who make up our Christian resources, who are agricultural workers, musicians, educators, mechanics and workers in many other areas I shall not stop to name. And these people, if the stigma were removed from being called a "former missionary"—which always hurts a returned missionary because it implies something which in most cases is not true—if this stigma were removed and these talented people could be sent by their denominations there to serve shoulder to shoulder with the wonderful people already there, Christianity could once again begin to make a major impact on international affairs around the world.

To be sure there are many, many reasons one may think of why some of these things can't be done. But we have a call from Christ to go into all the world and preach the Gospel, and to do it by every means at our command, and to send the people that will go out there and support them to the best of our ability, and to do less than our best, *today*, is to court disaster.

EIGHT

Factors in Our Favor

As a result of present world conditions, pertaining to the future of our Western Christian culture in general, and to our Christian mission program in particular, certain favorable factors may be observed:

1. There is a new pioneer spirit abroad in the world, which seems to have been bred from the spirit of despair on the part of a great many Christian leaders of this and the past generation. This new spirit matches the rise of nationalism and infiltrates it on every side. As a consequence, the established state churches are being questioned and challenged as never before.

2. There is a new spirit of assessment of the methods early-day Christianity used to permeate the world.
   a. Establishment of churches.
   b. The use of channels heretofore ignored.
   c. Exploitation of the soft spots.
   There are indications on every hand that should the militant spirit of early-day Christianity break out, a ripening world would experience a revival on a scale never before seen.

3. A renewed study of mission methods is taking place by the present leadership of mission boards. The result should and will be an updating of methods and a resurgence of interest and concern.

4. There is ·a firm conviction on the part of many responsible leaders in government, as well as business and church circles, that New Testament Christianity is the only answer, and they seem to be willing to try it or see it tried.

5. A realization on the part of those who are *not* religious-minded that regardless of their own personal indifference, they do live in a world grown so small that no nation on earth is so far removed that they can afford to ignore its capacity as a friend or as an enemy. But they and we know that only leaders of Christian concern can bring into harmonious relationship the nations of the world, if such can ever be done.

For centuries Christianity has been imprisoned. Imprisoned by patterns of thought and conduct conceived and operated under certain circumstances which were actually alien to the original spirit of the faith. Why they worked as well as they did is a tribute to the tremendous innate power which the faith contained.

Properly stated, these imprisoning and limiting patterns are:

1. Institutionalization at the expense of New Testament evangelization.

2. Static commitment to an area at the expense of mobility led by the Holy Spirit. (Permanent involve-

ment in spite of changing circumstances made apparent by sudden unexpected acceptability of the Gospel in hitherto closed or at least hard situations.)

3. Principal dependence on highly trained personnel rather than maintaining minimum standards based on the New Testament requirements of genuine conversion and a divine calling that was not necessarily for life.

It is immediately recognized by the author that each of these suggestions will meet overwhelming criticism and resistance. Yet two things are crystal clear, and people who disagree must explain them away before they can prove their case. These two things are:

1. Centuries of effort involving these three principles have not resulted in worldwide success.
2. Yet, when these principles are checked against the first hugely successful years of expansion of Christianity, hardly a trace of them can be found.

If these two facts can be explained away, then the case for present methods will be immeasurably strengthened.

Look at number one, "Institutionalization at the expense of Holy-Spirit-led mobility." Church growth has always resulted from hard work among responsive people. The Holy Spirit appeared to Paul, in a dream, as a man from Macedonia crying, "Come over and help us." Instantly Paul's future plans were amended. Westward he turned in the typical spirit of mobility of the early Christian and a rich harvest was the result. We are the inheritors of it. The total mobility of these people may again be illustrated by Peter's vision which led him to the Gentiles, or by Philip's following of the Spirit which led him to a desert place where the Ethiopian Eunuch was met and converted. This, of course, was the only meaning of the tenth chapter of Luke, as Christ sent out the seventy. "Carry no purse, no bag, no sandals; and salute no one on the road. Whatever house you enter, first say, 'Peace be to this house!' And if a son of peace is there, your peace shall rest upon him; but if not, it shall return to you. And remain in the same house, eating and drinking what they provide, for the laborer deserves his wages; do not go from house to house. Whenever you enter a town and they receive you, eat what is set before you; heal the sick in it and say to them, 'The kingdom of God has come near to you!'" (Luke 10:4–10, RSV.)

Notice also Paul's reaction to rejection by the Jews as described in the thirteenth chapter of Acts, verses 46–49, RSV: "And Paul and Barnabas spoke out boldly, saying, 'It was necessary that the word of God should be spoken first to you. Since you thrust it from you, and judge yourselves unworthy of eternal life, behold, we turn to the Gentiles. For so the Lord has commanded us, saying, 'I have set you to be a light for the Gentiles, that you may bring salvation to the uttermost parts of the earth.' And when the Gentiles heard this, they were glad and glorified the word of God; and as many as were ordained to eternal life believed. And the world of the Lord spread throughout all the region."

See again Paul's letter to the Galatians, where he described for them the events at the great conference in the Church at Jerusalem. "And when they perceived the grace that was given to me, James and Cephas and John, who were reputed to be pillars, gave to me and Barnabas the right hand of fellowship, that we should go to the Gentiles and they to the circumcised" (Galatians 2:9, RSV).

These and other passages point out the easy fluidity of movement that was the method the Holy Spirit chose to spread the Gospel. Since there are as many people today who are not believers as then, and even more, then have we some new commandment that teaches us to arrive on a scene of missionary activity and "dig in" as it were with institutions of all kinds? Institutions cannot be "bad" per se. Of course not! But institutions tie down people who could otherwise be moved by the Spirit to areas where a ready spirit of acceptability might be loose among the people, and the results may be tenfold what would have come, if ever, from the highly expensive, immobile institution which in ninety per cent of the cases is actually struggling to exist. The time and place of institutionalized Christianity arrive sooner or later on every successful mission field. In fact, some governments where mission work is conducted require school work of the missionaries as a basis of the permission to carry on their work.

But the institution we were commanded to establish was the New Testament Church. And the coin of the Kingdom consists only of saved souls and New Testament Churches. That's what Paul "majored" in, and that was the primary program of New Testament Christianity. Kindergartens, grade schools, high schools and hospitals are sponsored by many and varied denominations around the world, yet, even here on the home front, not one of these institutions forms a major part of the soul-winning program of most evangelical denominations. Why? Well, more than likely, it is because secular agencies supply the need to a large extent. Secondly, they are far too expensive to enter into along with the other evangelistic programs to which we are already committed. Also, it is generally recognized that though the results of this kind of work are immeasurably valuable, they are rather slim numerically. It all works out to the proving of this formula: Mission schools equal maximum expense plus maximum personnel plus minimum results.

There is another factor. If institutions are to be nourished and cherished, they will do better to have their roots in native or local establishments rather than in "foreign." In other words, let the indigenous churches establish their own schools and hospitals, with a minimum of assistance from outside, so that the thus-established institutions can draw upon local loyalties for their support and future growth. It has been thus in our own land. Many of our greatest Christian institutions started in log cabins or in someone's home. The ensuing loyalties have carried them through fire, flood and war, and they have grown great. To try to substitute another method on mission fields may actually have weakened our forward thrust instead of strengthening it.

Now look at number two: "Static commitment to an area in spite of changing circumstance (other than war) made apparent by an unexpected acceptability of the Gospel in a hitherto untouched, previously closed or formerly difficult area."

Here has been a proof of point number one. While large numbers of mission personnel have struggled in widely separated areas under adverse circumstances, a sudden breakthrough has been accomplished by some missions under none other than Holy Spirit leadership. As a boxer looks for a weakness in his opponent's defense, so we look for a place in Satan's defense where unexpected good fortune might attend our work. Glowing reports have come in, for instance, about the successful operation of the Spirit of God in the hearts of the people of Brazil. It is said by those who have witnessed it that seldom before has there been seen such ready acceptance as is going on there now. Years of labor (and the good work of some fine institutions, we are ready to admit) have been coupled with the moving of the Holy Spirit, and revival and church establishment are taking place on a magnificent scale. Exploiting this "soft spot" should now be the order of the day. Upon the first evidences of its appearance, selected personnel from other areas, where no breakthrough is in sight would now be moved in. (Not of necessity, of course, as was the case upon the Communist sealing-off of China, when great numbers of fine missionaries were moved into the Philippines and perhaps Japan.)

Moved in under these stirring circumstances, the gain in the highly active field would offset any loss in the static areas from which every spare person was removed. Here again the earnest critic will speak. He will remind us of the unstable missionary who worked a while in an area of a certain country, made many mistakes and "fumbled the ball," and then irresponsibly moved away to a new spot to renew his ill-starred efforts. The results of his misadventure had to be remedied by his responsible brethren who were near by or came in later. "Such cases," they say, "are worse than if no effort had been begun at all." We counter that objection with a reminder to our critic that we are speaking of Holy-Spirit-led men and women of God, not hop-skip-and-jump, johnny-come-lately do-gooders, sincere though they may be.

It is not news to any man of God that the Holy Spirit often leads us to attempt work for Him which results in failure. If this were not so, then every soul to whom we have spoken about Christ, to whom we believed we were sent, would have been converted. Sadly enough, such was and is not the case. Even Jesus counseled the seventy, "But whenever you enter a town and they do not receive you, go into its streets and say, 'Even the dust of your town that clings to our feet, we wipe off against you; nevertheless know this, that the kingdom of God has come near.'" (Luke 10:10–11, RSV).

A case in point of the sudden acceptability of the Gospel on the part of a hitherto difficult area is Nigeria. The willingness of the people there to receive the Gospel has been so astounding in recent years that churchmen who have worked there or have been there report that fifty churches a year could be established if a preacher of suitable caliber could be found for each one. Such was not always the case. A former medical missionary to Ogbomosho, Nigeria, stated that the language problem coupled with the tribal religions of the people at one time constituted an apparently insurmountable problem. And then came the inexplicable (inexplicable, that is, if we ignore the leadership of the Holy Spirit) breakthrough. Today this area actually cries for more and more assistance. The story on Formosa constitutes another similarly thrilling saga of Christian history.

The whole point is this: with the limited funds and personnel which Christian denominations contend with everywhere today, regrouping to exploit weak or "soft spots" should be the immediate action of a truly militant Christianity. When the "left flank and the center remain solid and irresistible, and the right flank begins to give, pull forces that can be spared from left and center and throw them into the right with sufficient force to result in a breakthrough, after which one may surround the enemy from the rear and destroy him or capture him at will." Thus wrote a military commander to his student officers. And, with necessary modifications, the same tactics might well work in the "science" of Christian warfare against darkness and ignorance.

It all boils down to a simple formula, and that is "priority of response." This should be the criterion for assignment or reassignment of money and personnel.

Though much more, with present-day illustrations, could be written to support this statement, let us move on to point number three.

"Principal dependence on highly trained personnel rather than determining to maintain previously decided minimum standards based on the New Testament requirements of genuine conversion, and a divine calling that was not necessarily for life."

Here the critic will find great fault. He will tell you, and rightly, that the highest standards have not always been high enough. He will properly point to specific instances where the work on certain fields was terribly set back as a result of unforeseen weakness which appeared in the life or character of an otherwise highly trained and carefully selected missionary. He will remind us that in almost every case, genuine conversion and divine calling were easily apparent, yet they did not prevent the "apostasy."

Of course, he is right. West Point-trained Aaron Burr

proved to be a traitor to his country. Judas failed and fell. Ananias and Sapphira provided embarrassing chapters in Christian history. But the greatness of God and the power of His command kept the places in the line filled when traitors fell by the wayside. These we have always had with us and always will. Nor would we deliberately subject the cause of the Gospel to any embarrassment except those that are absolutely unavoidable. But the critic is requested to sit back and listen for a moment.

Recently, a great missionary leader summed up the situation by saying, "We are in danger of losing our present-day generation." His statement, added to those of men in every walk of life, reminds us that in the next ten years we face a crisis greater than the world has hitherto faced. This is no false danger. This is no cry of "wolf." There is a genuine, complete emergency. And the next few years will tell the story. Churchill summed up a similar situation for the Allied Forces in general and the English people in particular when he spoke of the threatened strike of Hitler at the British Isles by saying, "Let us so conduct ourselves that it will be said of us by future generations, 'This was their finest hour.'"

This call to superhuman exertion must be sounded in our day by all men of Christian conscience who have accurately estimated the situation the Christian forces face. Now, if these facts are true, and they are, then emergency measures are certainly in order! These emergency measures should be adopted by us only so long as the present desperate situation faces us. And one result of lowering standards to a previously decided minimum is that the near one hundred per cent effectiveness of the present mission efforts would be dropped to seventy-five per cent effectiveness or even fifty per cent! We contend, however, that fifty per cent effectiveness would be better than zero per cent, which we now actually have in hundreds of strategic places. If a nation is challenged as our nation was and as England was in 1941, we call to the colors men and women whom we would have previously left untouched. The esprit-de-corps of the pre-World War II Marine Corps was one hundred per cent higher than it was when it had to swallow thousands of "civilian soldiers" who were suddenly inducted. But they took Guadalcanal nevertheless!

We cannot, from our vantage-point, decide which standards might best be lowered, and which must not be lowered under any circumstances. But certain suggestions in other areas, which are related, which would serve as to ways and means of making possible an all-out assault on the lost men of our world, might not be out of order.

Since early Christianity traveled remarkably by way of the Roman military establishment, something similar might happen today. The United States maintains one of the largest armed-service establishments in the history of the world. In that huge network of men on almost every continent on earth, there are thousands of Christian men and women, as well as excellently trained chaplains. These people, while on the payroll of the United States, could serve as witnesses for Christ and consequently present a better ambassadorship of America to the world. At present, however, this area of service possibility has not been correlated with the foreign mission efforts of evangelical denominations. This, of course, is not true of the Catholic youth in our armed services. In

countless cases, they are serving in *official* capacities in
Catholic Churches in the area where they serve Uncle Sam.

Secondly, early Christianity was marvelously spread by
the efforts of the traveling merchant. Some of their names
are recorded in the New Testament as timeless reminders of
this "network for Christ." Dorcas, Priscilla and Drusilla,
Philemon and even Paul, the tent maker, and others.

The only present-day counterpart of the traveling "lay
preacher" is the individual employed by worldwide business
concerns and stationed in countries where we now have
mission efforts under the guidance of small but efficiently
trained mission personnel. Not only do we have some now
who occupy such places, who are not being used as they
should and could, but we can provide a program of infiltration of worldwide forces with capable Christian laymen and
women in a hundred different capacities. By setting up a de-
partment within our present mission boards, we could locate
young people of Christian dedication, who are training to be
scientists, geologists, teachers, engineers, etc. Then we could
form a catalogue of United States businesses who operate in
these various chosen areas and investigate their needs in
future specialized fields. Then, over the years, we could place
with these companies these trained young people, in the
openings which would occur, and do two things of significant
importance at the same time—provide the United States with
good "ambassadors," the kind who would not turn out to be
"ugly Americans," and at the same time provide dedicated
assistance to local missionary forces and indigenous churches.
This program would not be unique to us. The Catholic
Church has practiced such "job placement" for almost fifty

years. It has done this in the many fields of "mass communication" in America to the point where no single newspaper, magazine, television network or movie studio does not have selected people serving in selected places. It has also done as well in foreign affairs of government and business. Such a program on a massive scale is long overdue among the evangelicals. (We understand that some Protestant Church bodies have been doing this in recent years, but on a comparatively small scale.) The time for the program is ripe for each church body and the cost can be easily borne from presently available funds.

But of even more importance is the possibility of using full-time missionary personnel who have not been committed to a lifetime service. This has been dealt with in a previous chapter, but an additional word here will not be out of place. Hardly a church in America of any missionary zeal would fail to have at least one truly dedicated Christian with specialized training who would, if given the opportunity, be glad to serve for a limited period in needy areas. There are language teachers, already trained in many instances, whose love for Christ would make it consistent and possible for them, in these days of crisis, to offer themselves on a definite time-basis as missionary servants. Doctors, many of whom engage in a type of Christian ministry already in their service to the charity patient, would be able to relieve for a furlough-period, the full-time lifetime doctor serving on some mission field. From the Alumni Bulletin of the School of Medicine, at Oklahoma University, Norman, Oklahoma, came the following story: "Mercy journey has been completed by Dr. Samuel T. Moore, Oklahoma City, the fourth

American orthopedist to travel to Jerusalem at his own expense to help with medical care of Jordan refugees. Some 100 orthopedic surgeons have pledged to succeed each other at volunteer duty for one month each. The project is the brainchild of the International Orthopedic Letters Club, first organized ten years ago."

Builders, architects, publicists and students of journalism, agronomists and veterinarians, and scores of other specialists might be willing to offer themselves as "civilian soldiers" of the Cross in time of worldwide emergency. The churches from which these people came would find themselves personally involved for the first time in real Christian missions. The results of such personal involvement on their part would be impossible to predict. The standards would be lowered? Yes, to think otherwise would be foolish. But isn't some service better than no service? Didn't Christ call men to serve Him who were limited in their capacities? And though few, if any of them, became "missionary heroes," they did serve to the glory of God. Perhaps it was some of these of whom the writer of Hebrews spoke when he wrote: "Who through faith conquered kingdoms, enforced justice, received promises, stopped the mouths of lions, quenched raging fire, escaped the edge of the sword, won strength out of weakness, became mighty in war, put foreign armies to flight. Women received their dead by resurrection. Some were tortured, refusing to accept release, that they might rise again to a better life. Others suffered mocking and scourging, and even chains and imprisonment. They were stoned, they were sawn in two, they were killed with the sword; they went about in skins of sheep and goats, destitute, afflicted, ill-treated" (Hebrews 11:33–37, RSV). To whom was the Gospel writer speaking but to these stalwart and available lay people of the Kingdom when he wrote, "I appeal to you therefore, brethren, by the mercies of God, to present your bodies as a living sacrifice, holy and acceptable to God, which is your spiritual worship." (Roman 12:1, RSV). We'll never know until we give them the chance. No time could be more ripe for a trial than the present.

Another factor in our favor, not mentioned hitherto, is the worldwide interest in the English language and things American. Upon recent visits of the author to Europe and Asia and South America, no single matter of interest was impressed on him more than the fact that English is at least the unofficial international language. Much more so, in fact, than the French language ever was in its diplomatic heyday. The time has arrived when an English-speaking traveler may go to almost any country on earth, be addressed in his own language when debarking, order his hotel room and his meals in English, and usually be able to converse with someone near by as he enjoys his luxuries and his food. Such is becoming increasingly more common every day. Who can measure the impact of this fact upon the modern mission movement? Growing interest in American medicine, books, film, clothes, food, machinery, anything we produce, is eagerly manifested by the peoples of the world. They wear our clothes, follow our fashions, eat our food, listen to our music on records or by radio, go wild over our musicians, and talk our language.

They have copied our Constitution, borrowed our weapons, used our farming methods, planted our seed, listened to our political leaders. The one thing we have not exported on a massive scale, nor shared successfully with all of them is the Gospel. This is the one thing we possess in abundant quantity which the U.S.S.R. does not possess at all. But, alas, present plans do not include a program which could really succeed in doing this. The question that has risen among many observers is, "Suppose using the present plan of operation, we were to double, actually double the present amount of money going to foreign missions, and double the number of missionaries now on the mission fields, what effect would this have on world conditions?" In other words, is the problem really more money and more personnel, or is that only *half* of the problem?

Is the other half of the problem the finding of new methods to reach the world in these changing times?

Firstly, we know that there are millions and millions of people in the world who do not know how to read or write. Dr. Frank Laubach has dramatized this fact and has provided a means by which it can be partially overcome in a relatively short time and with limited funds. We know that the knowledge of reading, when taught with Bible stories and actual scriptures, provides a man with something he can easily pass on to others. The "Laubach Plan" has been proven on a worldwide basis; yet it is not a major part of any evangelical mission program today. In many cases, it is not even a minor part.

Secondly, the use of radio as a means of reaching the masses is a sadly neglected medium of preaching. In India, there are over twelve million radio receiving sets. Though there are 400 million Indians, it is still hard to believe that anyone would overlook an audience of twelve million listeners. Similar groups can be found in every civilized country. National boundaries are not recognized by the Gospel-carrying radio wave; thus radio provides a means to overcome the wickedness of a nationalistic dictator with Communist tendencies, who refuses to allow Christian missionaries in his country. However, with the exception of several "Christian Radio Stations" (which by their very name take away some of their effectiveness in reaching millions), there is no organized "Voice of America" type of ministry in all the world. Imagine a "Voice of Peace" radio program, beamed over commercial and Christian stations, several hours every day, with messages of personal witnessing by laymen as well as preachers. Imagine the possibilities of a bombardment of Communist countries with daily broadcasts throughout the world by shortwave and standard band. Imagine applying every subtlety which we possess in "psychological warfare" in getting the message out to the ends of the earth! Here is the instrument, perfected and ready, and the enemy uses it today to harass and disturb or lull and rock to sleep the peoples of the world. Torrents of lies, half-lies and twisted truths pour out in every language which men speak.

But is Christianity fighting back? Is there any movement on foot to mount a giant radio offensive with the Gospel of Christ and the unadorned word of God in every language of man? None! Not really, though some valiant independent efforts have been made. Here is an area of service in these changing times that has not been used. Surely we have seen that there are many factors in our favor by which we might stem the tide of Communism's advance, and even reverse the flow, so that in the wisdom and mercy of God and by and through the leadership of the Holy Spirit, we might preach Christ the Saviour to our neighbors in our small, small world. "For since, in the wisdom of God, the world did not know God through wisdom, it pleased God through the folly of what we preach to save those who believe" (I Corinthians 1:21, RSV).

NINE

Reasons for Concern

As in all matters of a pioneer nature, there are certain factors that require thought and caution. No one is suggesting that we "junk" the present system of programs on the local church level or within the bodies of our various mission boards. None of us could be any more concerned with finding new and successful methods of accomplishing the task of world revival than those who are engaged in this pursuit by divine calling. By sacrifice and heroic effort all boards and missions are seeking the answers. There have been numerous surveys and studies conducted by skilled and trained minds. Hundreds of trips abroad have been conducted by secretaries of missions, delegations of ministers and groups of laymen and professional men such as doctors. All are eager to do a better job. The very fact of their studies and concern indicate that they realize we must redouble our efforts and perfect our methods before it is too late.

Mr. Billy Graham returned from his African crusade to present suggestions as to how he believed improvement could occur. His report included high and sincere and deserved praise for the work he observed being done in that continent. He and others declare there should be caution and careful study coupled with any intensified program. But all agree we must move swiftly and on a much vaster scale if we are to meet Africa's need in these days of rising nationalism and increased tempo among the leaders of Mohammedanism.

The first ventures of what we call the modern mission movement were of a necessity conducted with extreme caution. How would tribes react to this new faith? What methods should be used? What kind of personnel should be chosen? What was the language and could it be written? Who would provide Bibles and could there ever be an indigenous church that would be completely self-supporting? These and thousands of other questions had to be answered. Now, in the twentieth century, the answers are in—enough of them for us to proceed in a new kind of attack. But this new approach will raise new and hitherto unsuspected questions.

Fortunately, the leadership we have today is even better fitted to meet the issues and solve the problems. The job is to get the masses of Christian laymen of America and the world to "move off center" and begin this new era of modern missions. We've gone from the age of the industrial revolution of the seventeenth and eighteenth centuries into the jet and atomic and space ages of the twentieth century. We must see to it that the methods of missions keep up with the swift-moving events in our world.

The following major question will certainly have to be faced and solved before much progress can be made:

Can Christian people be depended upon to be mature enough in their spiritual balance to face the facts of

mission-failure from the beginning of their denominations' mission activities to the present moment? This fact
of failure cannot be overemphasized. For there are
some who believe that should the whole story be revealed, dollars spent per souls won from the world, they
would seriously consider dropping the whole matter.
("Souls from the world" refers to those won and baptized other than the annual "crop" of children of
already-Christian homes.)

By way of summary here are some factors that demand
caution:

1. We must know whether the American people can
    ever again be gripped with the power of an idea
    again.
2. Are the Christian people of our denominations pre-
    pared with enough information and are our churches
    organized properly to give support for carrying out
    on a permanent basis the kind of massive drama
    which this new approach to world missions would
    demand?
3. Are we prepared to meet the violent opposition such
    a program would face from such countries as Saudi-
    Arabia? Such opposition would not only come from
    various anti-Christian nations, but from within our
    government and within United States business cir-
    cles as well. Is the Gospel "the power of God unto
    salvation unto the Jew first and also to the Greek"?
    Our spiritual forebearers thought so, and were not
    deterred by resultant opposition to their efforts. Are

we to be intimidated or not? Under just what circumstances does "go ye" apply and under which ones does it not apply?

4. Such a program would demand a closer coordination of representatives of the various denominations involved in mission areas. ·That coordination would have to begin with mission boards here in America first. Is it possible to subjugate the differences in church government on at least a temporary basis to the extent necessary in order to face up to the emergency of this decade? And would such "compromise" result in future weaknesses and excesses of "power-politics" among churchmen to make the whole idea too risky? Can American spiritual leaders forget "empire building" long enough to work together without embarrassing organizational entanglements arising? History will hold us responsible for the answer we give.

Of course, there are some related matters that demand extreme caution and prayerful thought. One is this: is it possible that the church-state separation which we so anxiously safeguard could be abrogated by any kind of worldwide advance on this scale? I don't know. That is something that would have to be very carefully studied. For it would be impossible for the Christians of America to plan and promote and carry out such an all-out program without, to one degree or another, involving our country and its foreign policy and international relations. Whether these involvements would prove harmful or not can only remain to be seen.

For this and other reasons, I think that the committee of laymen, ministers and businessmen referred to earlier should be chosen to enter into a permanent study of these matters and report back to their various denominations year by year on their studies. This committee would have some sort of rotation of its membership so that other men and women could be added to it from time to time—people of national or international reputation who are prepared to recommend and discuss strategy and planning for this kind of evangelistic approach.

Furthermore, we shall face dangers when we attempt to mobilize our forces on this scale. For in the mobilization of great numbers of personnel we may find ourselves lowering the quality of our missionaries. This, of course, could be very, very hazardous. But it is also possible for us to have such high qualifications that we turn down many who may be equipped and called of God to go. When I was a student, I walked down the aisle of my own seminary and surrendered my life to foreign missions only to be told that in spite of my call and my education, I was too old. I was only thirty-two at the time! The truth of the matter is that there's a question in the minds of many of the missionaries themselves as to whether the present age qualification is a real factor or not in our work.

Another reason for caution is that the use of lay-workers on a short time basis may weaken our thrust. This is very possible. But let us remind ourselves that our foreign mission boards already use "contract" or short-term workers in some areas of their far-flung work today. It's entirely possible that this could be further broadened to include large numbers of people who are equipped and talented and called, but not qualified according to present strict standards. But having been carefully screened first, they might render valuable service for a comparatively brief time in spite of certain shortcomings.

Another question arises: is our Christian culture prepared to accept this responsibility on a worldwide permanent basis? And, in answer to that question, I'd say that if our nation has agreed to accept the responsibility of guarding the freedom of all men in the world, and it has, then I see no reason why the Christian people in our churches in America cannot say to one another and to the world, "We will share the spiritual responsibilities of preaching Christ to the world on a permanent basis. And we'll do so to the best of our ability."

Another factor of concern stems from the non-Christian nations of the world such as Saudi-Arabia, who will violently oppose any move of this type. Such protests have always been raised, but they did not deter our early Christian brethren. If there is any actual deterrent anywhere, let's test it and see its strength.

There is some question in some circles whether America can ever again be gripped with an idea that will affect this world's destiny—ideas as great as those expressed in our Declaration of Independence and our Bill of Rights. Articles and statements from commentators in magazines recently assert that America is morally and spiritually adrift. We have no purpose, no cause, no direction, they say. Headed nowhere except for destruction. They indicate that it is impossible for us to be challenged by a world in need.

This isn't so! Not only is it not so, but the charge of spiritual bankruptcy is being pressed by our enemies, not by our friends. Americans travel around the world and return to the United States after two-, three- or four-week trips repeating statements such as these; they do not come from personal observation of international affairs, but are picked up from Communist-inspired propaganda in newspapers and elsewhere. Actually the true attitude of the people of the world toward our country might best be characterized by the immense crowds that gathered around the car of our president as he drove from country to country in his recent visits across the world. We're not the most hated nation in the world. But . . . we are the most watched and imitated nation in the world. And the world gets furious when we let them down, as we often do with some disgraceful event in our national life. For they look to us to set an example of behavior. We have the thing they need and they know it, and they wait with empty hands and empty hearts for us to give it to them. There must be, there *has* to be men and enough money to meet the challenge of our world. Else it will be said of us as it was said of Thomas Dewey when he was defeated for the presidency of the United States: "He managed to snatch defeat from the jaws of victory."

TEN

Race Against Time

THREE WORDS CHARACTERIZE THE DAYS IN WHICH WE LIVE: Time, Speed, Emergency. If what we see, read and hear is true, then no objection can be valid against these terms of description. These, indeed, seem to be the ideas that brought Christ into the world. "But when the time had fully come, God sent for his Son" (Gal. 4:4, RSV), the scripture says. Accordingly Paul's ministry was carried out against a frame of reference like ours. Paul seemed to live in the dimension of intensity. When a sense of divine mission takes hold of a man or a generation, time becomes of the essence, speed becomes the identifying mark, and emergency the characterizing attitude. One cannot hold a newspaper in one hand and a Bible in the other and not be compelled to action if he believes what he reads in both.

The time when there was time enough is gone. Whatever it is in the world that is moving, it is really moving! It isn't giving us time. If Christianity needs much more time to accomplish its end, it's through.

Look at this land of ours and see it as an island of plenty in an ocean of misery. It contains the greater part of the earth's productive wealth and we experience the consequences of that wealth. Simple things like bathtubs and toothbrushes. Complex things such as electrical power and technological know-how. We have been extremely successful in telling the world of our wealth. Our magazines and our movies are read and viewed in the most backward areas of human existence. The people there see the pictures and see the sights provided for them through various means of mass communication. They see them and they want them. They see no reason why they can't have material goods.

They suppose that if they had their national freedom, then all these things would soon be theirs. Luxuries grow on trees, and wealth and material possessions are a natural fruit of national independence. Here and there all over the world, men have thrown off colonialism in one form or another, and then waited for the miracle to take place. Of course, it didn't happen. Instead, they had even less. Disillusionment set in and eventually anger and desperation. Pulling one's self up by one's own bootstraps is often thought of as too hard. "There must be an easier way," they say.

And Communism steps in to assure them there is. To most of these people, rising as it were from economic slavery, Communism is not a political way of life. Frankly, many students of world affairs say that leaders in these backward nations, newly free, couldn't care less about Communism's long-term consequences. At the moment they tend to grasp Communism in their collective hands as a burglar's tool with which they intend to "jimmy" open the window and doors of plenty of the free world and take what they need. Ghana, Burma, Thailand, Indonesia, Ceylon and on and on make up the list of those who have been thus misled.

Then comes the backwash. Then comes the dreaded day

of opening their eyes to realize they have not bettered themselves. Instead, they have sold themselves into a form of
slavery far worse than anything they had ever dreamed. The
Communists have used the propaganda of our wealth against
us in the war of ideas and words. Now they attack with new
fury. "Let us compete." They tell the young, newly freed
nations, "Look at our sputnik. Look how far we've come in
only forty-three years while America has had generations.
Yet already we out-produce them in the missile race." They
are making loans and selling their machines and providing
engineering assistance, on a scale that almost matches ours.
They say, "We will out-produce America in every area of
need. Thus our way is better than their way."

Now uncommitted nations sit on the fence; neutralism
forms their principal international policy. But all thinking
men know a nation cannot remain balanced between the
two "worlds" in which we live. Nature will not permit such
an equilibrium to exist. A nation will tumble into one camp
or the other. With two-thirds of the world composed of colored people, and with the racial issue as their text, the Communists are capitalizing on our problems in this area. With
the rising tide of nationalism among the multiplying millions
of people in these underprivileged areas of the world,
pressing their faces against the windowpanes of our nation,
seeking all the food, clothes and luxuries we enjoy, they
must feel as a little hungry boy feels who looks in a bakery
window on a cold winter night. "We want what you have,
we don't want to wait." In the face of this condition, how
can we afford to cling to the philosophy of "gradualism" in
world missions? There was a time when that policy was
fine. That time is gone. As all things move swiftly today,

so must we move swiftly. There is an emergency facing our Christian people. This is no time to haggle over how much and when, or else it will be too little too late.

We are outnumbered, and far too often we are out-maneuvered. Yet the non-political masses of the world look primarily to us for help. We have helped them in many, many ways. But almost every foreign-aid program into which we have entered has been characterized by three things:

1. Great opposition from large numbers of our own people;
2. Waste, corruption and Communist infiltration have entered into the program of distribution;
3. Russian promises to do better with no "capitalistic strings of imperialistic slavery" attached.

Books could be written on the good intentions of the American people to help their neighbors, and the subsequent torpedoing of those intentions by Americans on one hand and Communists on the other. These are perilous times, and the demand for action is urgent.

The blind spot of most religious leaders consists of the failure to realize that our world is on the move. Tremendous forces are being brought to bear on world problems. And entire communities of nations are the target of these movements. For an example, the program of the International Bank for Reconstruction and Development, more generally referred to as the World Bank. This organization, with vast resources of money and talent, has ranged over the earth looking for places where needy people can find the needed money to improve their lot. This World Bank, through its president, Eugene R. Black, has made it clear to the whole watching world that the challenge for world peace lies in some other field besides arms. With a billion and a half people living on a starvation level, and with the world experiencing a population explosion without precedent, the simple fact stands out that poverty and human need must be met and satisfied or all else for which we stand is gone.

Now, for a pitifully short time the gap between world need and Christian Western Civilization's ability to help can be closed. Step by step, plans and procedures and supplies of men, material and the spirit of dedication can be rallied, trained, stockpiled and distributed. And, matching the economic help given by great foundations and private banking facilities, as well as government resources, the Christian community can gain tremendous respect in its own eyes as well as in the eyes of the world. Somehow there must be a way to motivate this action. Somewhere there must be a man or a group of men who can galvanize our people into forthright action immediately. We cannot afford to wallow in the slough of despair or despond, while the more vigorous but less spiritual forces of the world step into the vacuum of starvation and human need.

In addition, it must be recognized, that no matter how inventive Big Business, i.e., the World Bank, can be, there are areas in which it cannot work. In most instances these are the areas where the Christian forces can call into play their unique talents.

A. The explanation of capitalism in Christian terms abroad and the insistence on the home front that capitalism abroad behave in a Christian manner.

B. The presentation of international problems to the folks at home in understandable terms, so that the foreign-aid program of our country becomes a nation-wide act of compassion, rather than "a poorly understood program of seeming boondoggling, tax wasting, and the worldwide giveaway slush fund of a money-flush Congress."

C. It can interpret in terms of compassion and love the assistance of the Western World to the people who are being helped.

D. It can counteract Communist propaganda by being on the spot when food and supplies arrive, thus defeating the Reds when they attempt to change the "USA" on the stacks of supplies and the sacks of wheat to "USSR" as documented correctly in the best-seller, *The Ugly American*.

There have been times when processes of political and economic growth took place in "new ground." This is one of the things which cause the Declaration of Independence and the Constitution of the United States to stand out like pillars of history. They were new ideas and new concepts, born like blazing comets, to be viewed eagerly and reverently for ages to come. But the program of speeded-up missionary activity is not of this character. We know *what* to do, we know *how* to do it, we have a great sense of urgency all around us. The American ambassadors in many politically "hot" countries in the world plead for spiritual leaders in sufficient force to turn the tide. They plead for them now! Even the Secretary of State of the United States Government reveals his own sense of urgency in world affairs and spiritual matters in a speech delivered to the National Trade Council in New York, November 19, 1959.

"That competition is the life of trade," said Secretary Herter, "is a saying that has stood the test of time. Today we face a test no other society has ever fully met. How to make competition the life, not the death of nations.

"The problem is urgent as never before because of two facts. One is a revolutionary movement based on great and growing power, which seeks to polarize all international competition around social survival. The other is, that, hanging over this conflict, are the means of vast destruction."

Then Secretary Herter asked the question, "How can the great rivalry between political systems work itself out in the course of history without exploding into thermonuclear war?"

He named three rules for co-survival:

1. Set up ground rules.
   a. Common language
   b. Common interests
   c. Expand areas of worthwhile competition.
2. Meet the competition.
3. Faith in freedom.

Here is where this important address entered into the matters which we have been discussing. Mr. Herter said, "The problems which confront our nation and our free world call for every ounce of sacrifice and devotion that you and I, and all like minded men and women, can muster in the years ahead.

". . . Our main concern is not that the Soviets are trying to out-produce us in pigs, milk or steel. We rejoice at their progress to the extent that it makes for human betterment and for peace.

"What we need to fear most is the loss of our vision and sense of [direction] and of our belief in the eventual spread of democratic freedom to all peoples on our planet. In this we should have a faith as deep and intense as that of the most devoted disciple of Communism. We should, above all, demonstrate that faith in action."

Mr. Herter also said, "As against Marxist materialism, we uphold a universal humanism which stresses man's spiritual nature without ignoring his physical needs. We reject materialism as the main shaping force in human affairs, whether embodied in economic determinism, statism, or in any other system externally imposed upon the individual. We believe that the real dynamic of human life is inner spiritual force working in a cosmos ruled by Divine power, law and purpose."

Recalling statements of a similar vein made by leaders in every realm of secular life, since the closing scenes of World War II, one can come to only one honest conclusion. If man is a spiritual being, whose crucial needs of this hour can only be met with spiritual resources, and if there is a sense of emergency hanging over world affairs and even the existence of our nation, then we must find a way of matching the material and political contributions of our nation with dynamic and farsighted action in the spiritual realm on a scale never before attempted by the Christian people of the world. If there is the will, God will provide the way.

Our attitude might be clarified by the following experi-

ence of the author. During a visit to India, I got out of the
car and started to go over to a store. In a matter of moments,
although the guide had warned me, I was surrounded by at
least a hundred children and adults, all begging. The
guide began to shout, "Don't reach toward your pocket;
don't make any attempt to give anybody anything!" And
I realized that I was in danger, and I turned to get back
to the car. I tried to fight my way through the crowds. He
was still shouting, "Don't make any attempt to give them
anything; don't give anybody anything!" He explained to
me later that had I reached toward my pocket those on the
outside would have thought that those in the inner circle
were getting something from me and a riot would have begun and they would have killed me and stripped me and left
me there dead to take what I had. And he fought his way
through while the driver jumped out of the car and came
cursing and kicking the people aside and they got me back
in the car on the side of the driver.

As I got in and was trying to collect my wits, suddenly
I saw a man reach through the window of the cab and start
to drop a baby into my wife's lap. In the split second that
it happened I saw that the top of its head was a solid crust
of sores. The little child's eyes were closed. Whether it was
insensible or asleep I will never know. And in that moment
as he stuck it in, he said, perhaps in very poor English,
"Your baby!" and he dropped it into my wife's lap. The
guide turned around, pushed it back into his arms, hit him
across the face, cursed him, and at the same time the driver
gave the gas to the car and we drove away, almost hitting
some of the people. We drove off, both of us shocked to the

bottom of our hearts at what had happened in a matter of less than three minutes. I have never forgotten that baby or man. I don't know whether it is alive today, but it lives in my heart—"Your baby, your baby!" This is "our baby"— we cannot fail if we go with God.